SOUVENIRS
OF
TUSCANY

Yes, We Can Cook by Helen Dow Whiting.

SOUVENIRS
OF
TUSCANY

HELEN DOW WHITING

To Mac, with love—
Without you, none of this would have happened...

PRELIMINARIES

My father, Willard, was finely attuned to the appreciation of little anomalies. By his definition they are those little amusing or puzzling dilemmas which, he always said, "tickle one's ribs." He taught both Mac and me how much fun they are. We are sharply reminded of this special gift from him while experiencing Italy. As we roam through the city of Florence and the adjacent countryside of Tuscany, we delight in experiencing many. How much more poignant observing these little jokes and gentle razzing made being there for us, and they are our souvenirs of Tuscany.

To the casual eye these little episodes are part of everyday life so Italians tend to take them for granted. On the contrary they draw our attention. With their own momentum we see escapades starting to intrude on the surroundings that attract interest. Enjoying such trivia and sensing a development that may tickle our ribs, we stop to watch with keen anticipation. We are seldom disappointed.

꧁

At the start no one except ourselves notices. Occasionally we are the only observers, and what happens is a quiet, subtle moment. Another time the scene might be quite different.

꧁

Italians never loiter, but they are quite able to suspend their business to enjoy the moment so a more raucous episode might begin like this: A few curious souls and Mac and I perceive something is about to happen. With us they pause to observe thereby luring others to watch. Our small gathering attracts many bystanders. What is everybody gawking at? A crowd assembles to see. The entire neighborhood is alerted, some leaning out of apartment windows. Comments are heard, and suggestions generously offered. That encourages the most casual watcher to become a lively participant. Everybody has something to contribute. They do so loudly with various hand gestures. A boisterously friendly rhubarb.

ᘓ

This gentle bantering probably lasts only a few minutes. Without any apparent reason why, and whatever reason germinated the original cause, suddenly everything quiets down. Everybody resumes his own business. It appears nothing out of the ordinary has happened. It was a mere trivia in the course of an ordinary day—much like disappearing ripples on a pond.

ᘓ

Experiencing these little events is better than any photographs we could take. They depict so well the wonderful nature of the Italian psyche, the true essence of the Italian spirit. They are the totally honest, spontaneous reactions to the unexpected—that unusual something which has distracted and added spice to the day's serenity. For us they become the core in our enjoyment of living in Italy. We watch for them. Some are funny. Many are unbelievable. There are those which are plain absurd. Above all they are subtle. One must attune oneself to this environment to experience their happening.

ᘓ

A potpourri of these little episodes make up the bulk of this manuscript. I deliberately write in no particular sequence. Since they occurred unexpectedly in our daily life so they are scattered throughout the book. A more formally edited manuscript could not tell the story as it happened nor would it feel Italian.

℘

The time span starts in the fall of 1979 when we first visit Poggio Ramerino. This is Part I. We continue visiting Tuscany and other places in Italy frequently. It seems fun to include some of these episodes also, which is Part II, and brings us to the present.

℘

We keep talking about these trivial events. Why? And, why write about them?

Let's begin . . .

1ST PROLOGUE

N I N E T E E N   S E V E N T Y   N I N E

Aman and a woman are seated at the table adjoining ours. The headwaiter, outfitted in black trousers with gray stripes, black weskit and a black swallow-tailed jacket, greets them. With a big smile he presents the menus. We are lunching at the Excelsior Hotel in Florence, Italy.

"Fetch me a Martini and Rossi," growls the man brusquely, totally disregarding the menu, "and, her . . .," pointing to his wife, "she wants dry sherry."

"Of course, sir," bows the polite, smiling headwaiter and gives his assistant a slip of paper with the order. Moments later the waiter comes back carrying a tray with two glasses. He sets one down in front of the man and the other by the wife. The man takes a swallow and gags.

"This is a martini!" he exclaims loudly. "How's your sherry?" turning toward his wife, "too sweet?"

"No, just fine," she murmurs softly.

He snaps his fingers to signal the headwaiter. "I told you to bring Martini and Rossi. This is a martini! Here, take it away."

"Sorry, sir," the headwaiter says pleasantly, removing the offending glass from the table. He writes another order and hands it to his assistant, standing next to him. Seconds later the waiter reappears with a glass of red vermouth.

"But, I didn't order red vermouth!" fumes the man, his face becoming the color of the aperitif. "Can't your waiter get anything straight?" The wife leans over patting his arm to soothe him.

"I am so sorry, sir. You desire white vermouth, I think." The headwaiter now hovers near their table, but still smiles courteously.

"Yes, for God's sake. White vermouth—Martini and Rossi. That's what I am attempting to get." The man is abrupt and indiscreet.

Hastily white vermouth is brought. The man accepts it without a word of thanks. Swallowing a large gulp, he turns, snaps his fingers noisily, saying, "Bring the menus. We want lunch. Hope we don't have to wait long for that!"

Mac and I look at each other dumbfounded. In this pleasant, somewhat formal, dining room one does not expect such a furor. "What a tactless, grouchy man," we say to each other. "He is not exactly demeaning the waiters, but he's certainly an impertinent clod the way he bosses people around . . . The poor wife! Imagine the problems traveling

with him! Wouldn't you know he's an American?" Funny
how the American men seem to divide into two extremes, the
real loudmouths or the quiet-reserved. It's either or and
hardly any shades in between! And the American women are
even easier to spot. They are the ones wearing all the jewelry.
How they love glittery diamond rings, gold bracelets on the
arms, and an abundance of chain necklaces around their
necks. Makes them very conspicuous here. Doesn't help the
American image either. "Look at that! Aren't the Italian
waiters handling him with a polish? Still they maintain a
decorum in the room for the rest of us. Such diplomats!"

We continue eating, but keep being annoyed with that
man. It is bothersome to be seated near someone irritable.
We decide such testy behavior could be a deflated feeling of
self-worth, maybe stemming from his retirement. Newly
retired ourselves we can empathize with this, but his attitude
is the antithesis of how we feel. We are in the process of
planning a total change in our life. Choosing to be away from
symbols of the past, we are originating a new beginning for
ourselves.

Our sole objective for being in Tuscany is to look for a
place to lease. This is not common practice in 1979 Italy. We
are told any number of villas may be bought, but there are
few to rent. We have an appointment with the only real estate
agent we could find who handles rentals in and around the
city of Florence and the surrounding countryside of Tuscany.
She believes she has something interesting for our inspection.

7

Hopefully living here will not provoke the unpleasant response to the problems of a strange environment that it seems to be doing to that loudmouthed fellow American in the dining room. From what we can observe it is difficult to imagine Italy prejudicing anybody adversely.

℥

Finding a place to reside in the Tuscany area is a first step in our immediate retirement plans. We want to live here for a period of several months. We are intrigued with this particular locality. Former business trips to Italy had taken us to Milan and Livorno. Since there is little personal time in business traveling, the nearby city of Florence and its environs were bypassed. Now time is our own. It is a gift whose value we are only beginning to appreciate. We are excited by the freedom it offers us.

℥

While living here we plan to learn to speak Italian, savor the arts and architecture everywhere, meander through the Tuscan countryside and thoroughly explore the city of Florence. (Firenze is its lovely Italian name. Italians pronounce it "Fee-rain-zay.") We anticipate the daily pleasure of eating with joy. For us initiating such an adventure in this culture seems an irresistible dream come true, and one full of interesting challenges. What a fresh, new beginning for our life! Now on with our search for a comfortable villa . . .

PART

1

The property we are to look at is called Poggio Ramerino and is several miles away from Firenze. We arrange for a car with a driver to take us there. About twenty minutes after a twisty, curvy ride from the city, we turn onto a road leading to the site. Unpaved and so scantly graded, this road is deeply rutted, and our hired English chauffeur, Frederick Hand, fears his Mercedes will get mired in the mud. Even worse, he suspects it will be badly scraped on its underside by numerous bumps and potholes.

"Oh Sor," worries Fred loudly, "I'm not sure this is a good idea. Is this really the right route?" Like us he has never been here.

"Yes, Fred, it is. Keep going," encourages Mac, who is reading the map and guiding him.

§

A tall man, who stands with a military bearing, the steel blue eyed Frederick Hand was born in the Birmingham area of England. He dresses in a dark suit with a white shirt and dark tie but wears no chauffeur's hat on his gray head. He came to Italy as a soldier in the Second World War and fought with the British army all the way up the Italian peninsula. He particularly remembers the fierce battle of Poggibonsi. He met his Italian wife soon after the war, married her and has seldom been back to England. He has lived here some forty years, but still thinks of himself as an Englishman. He literally butchers the Italian language. Stopping at a toll booth he says to the ticket collector, "she voley oona reecheevoota," meaning, a receipt is needed. Even we who cannot understand Italian cringe at his pronunciation of "ci vuole una ricevuta."

§

"Y're certainly safe from the Russians har, Sor," mutters Fred as he gingerly steers the car.
"What can possibly be at the end of this miserable road?" I think to myself. "Can there be a villa of interest to us?"

§

About fifteen miles from Florence the last village we passed was Pozzolatico. Our map says the nearest town is Impruneta three miles ahead. We have turned off the highway onto this country road called via di Riboia. Besides being unpaved and bumpy, it is narrow, has numerous blind corners and no side shoulders. An automobile the size of Fred's takes up almost its entire width. There is no room for passing. Should a vehicle appear from the opposite direction, either it or Fred will have to back up to find a turnout so the other can go by. On either side of the road are lovely old olive groves among which are a few scattered houses. Apparently it is a community of small farms.

Suddenly two stone houses loom in front of us, the largest by far in the neighborhood, and abruptly the road disappears! We are puzzled as the map shows our destination is just ahead. Fred drives cautiously, and we discover the road goes between the houses. This gap curves slightly to the left and is extremely narrow. Fred must proceed with caution. If he makes the most trivial swerve, one or both sides of his limousine will be badly scratched by their roughly hewn stone walls. We hold our breath, as if this may help shrink the size of the car. Slowly, slowly he steers through without a single scrape. Benissimo, Frederico!

There is the villa Poggio Ramerino! It is visible a short distance up the road on the left: a two-storied, pinkish sandstone house with a small tower, nestled among silver leaf olive trees. It looks precisely as described to us. A high stone

13

fence along the road hides the rest of the property. We stop
at the entrance. Mac and I get out while Fred parks the car
in a small turnout made for that purpose.

🝮

Opening the gate, our real estate agent greets us. With a
big smile she leads the way through a garden onto the terrace.
What a panoramic view of the hilly countryside with villas
scattered here and there and the silhouettes of Firenze in a
hazy, distant background. The scene is beautiful as well as
peaceful and quiet. The sunshine is warm. We can hear birds
singing! Such a contrast from the hustle-bustle of the city.
Beside us grows a handsome rose garden filled with robust
plants. They are almost three feet tall and nearly mature
enough to burst into bloom. The leaves on the trees are bright
green, beginning to unfold. Along one side of the house is a
fig tree with some ripe fruit. Our agent picks one to eat.
Mounds of rosemary grow on the berms around the house.
We breathe the country air and savor being here.

🝮

"Ramerino is what we call rosemary, you know," she says,
noticing us looking at the rosemary and wanting us to
understand how the property came about its unusual name.
"Ramerino is really the archaic spelling of rosmarino."
"And, the word poggio? What is its meaning?" we ask.
"The dictionary defines poggio as a hillock or small hill,"

14

she answers.

"So we might call Poggio Ramerino, in English, Rosemary Hill!" We are excited by comprehending the Italian words.

"Si, that would be proper," she replies.

✥

Suddenly, totally shattering the serenity, around the corner of the house dashes a cat, closely followed by a young, rambunctious little boy, clad in short, short pants. He is perhaps four years old. His hair is dark black, and his cheeks are rosy red. He is after the cat, running as fast as his chubby legs will go. He is laughing and yelling at the same time. The cat stays a length or two ahead. The sturdy little boy is brandishing a pair of pruning shears. Dashing through the rosebushes, which are almost over his head, he is threatening to chop the tail off of that cat!

This is our introduction to Massimo, the son of the caretakers and his cat, Cina.

✥

This day when we inspect the inside of Poggio Ramerino, it had been unoccupied for several months. The furniture is askew with no pictures on the walls nor rugs on the floors. The terracotta colored slate floors are dirty and unswept. The curtains are drawn and hanging unevenly. Cobwebs have gathered in some corners. The whole effect is dark and

15

unattractive, but with a little ingenuity one can imagine developing it into a charming place to live. The floor plan both up and downstairs is well proportioned and spacious with plenty of windows for light and sunshine. While not a large villa there are many bedrooms and handsome, fully tiled bathrooms. It is built to last forever so strong its construction. We like what we see in spite of its disarray.

If we rent, we naively assume it our responsibility to make the place livable. Certainly we would rearrange the furniture. We usually do that wherever we stay, moving things around until they are harmonious to our eye. We assume the furnishings we see are the ones the owners will make available with the rental. There are few pieces, hardly enough for comfortable living, and they are not very attractive. We do note, if properly hung on their hooks, the living room curtains on the floor to ceiling windows are nicely made and of a pretty white beige color, a good neutral color.

౿

We find a corner to quietly talk by ourselves. We try to analyze why the living room is so unappealing. This is the central room, the core of the house, after all. If it cannot be made attractive, we reason, neither can the rest of the house. What does it lack besides better furniture? We ignore its obvious need to be cleaned. We do not include our agent in this discussion. How we might want the place to look is not a part of her leasing job.

౿

First, we miss seeing what Italians call arredi: odds and ends such as vases and knick-knacks, rugs and paintings, books and magazines—this sort of personal paraphernalia to strew about and make the ambiance seem more homey. We ponder aloud which and what of our accessories we might bring from home in the United States. Next, the furniture: To our eye it is a disaster! It looks like a mish-mash of broken discards from someone's attic. Nothing fits or blends. There apparently was no interior plan for arranging anything in the room. Can we remedy this?

We recall walking by two furniture stores in Florence stocked full of good-looking wicker pieces. There was everything from chairs to tables to beds. We know it is manufactured here and is available to purchase directly from the store. Some might be nice in this country environment. Should we think about working out a floor plan using it? No reason not to go in and have a look. We continue walking around the room observing, thinking . . . Seems like the walls need help too. In their great height they look bare and too severe even with the softening effect of the curtains. Perhaps we have some pictures at home to hang on them . . . Suddenly we feel a surge of excitement and a desire to bring Poggio Ramerino to life. Then and there we decide if the lease is reasonable, yes, we shall sign it. This villa seems a perfect place for us to live.

We are told Poggio Ramerino had been a working farmhouse, what the Italians call a casa colonica. We estimate it is between four and five hundred years old. This is somewhat difficult to determine because there is only one original wall, the outside curved one in the dining room. The entire structure was recently modernized, but originally it was one of the outpost houses around the estate property known as Riboia. The two large buildings which via di Riboia passes between when we squeezed Fred's limousine through were the main quarters of the estate.

⌘

The Poggio, our shortened version of its name, is two storied. When it was built, the downstairs was a stable for farm animals. People lived upstairs, maybe as many as twenty or thirty altogether. This is difficult to imagine since the space does not seem that large. The upstairs now has five bedrooms: three small ones with windows toward via di Riboia and another larger one with its own bath on the front side of the house, overlooking the garden and swimming pool. It has a wonderful view of distant Florence. The fifth is the master suite situated along the driveway side of the house. Its door opens into a sitting room. Two unusual things in this room are a fireplace along one wall and a shallow, stone sink on the opposite wall. These are from the original building. The room was the kitchen of the casa colonica. The fireplace has a huge opening. Pots for cooking would be hung over the fire on a heavy iron hand-wrought chain. There was plenty of space for the cook to stand and stir as well as alcoves on either side for persons to sit and be warm. This room is attractively arranged with a small comfortable sofa, upholstered in a lovely flowered English chintz with two identical chairs on either side in the same material. The wall facing is one of bookshelves filled with all sorts of reading material. (An album we discover has photographs of the renovation of this property. We see in detail the massive work done to make it habitable, obviously a formidable project.) Through this sitting room to the right is a large, somewhat formal bedroom with windows overlooking both the front terrace and driveway. On the left of the sitting room is a dressing room having two built-in clothes closets plus a large tiled bathroom. Adjacent the fireplace wall in the dressing room area is a short, steep stairwell. It goes up to the tower. We assume this is a small room, but do not take time to investigate it.

Outside this suite in the hallway is a massive carved stone staircase. It leads downstairs to the entryway of the Poggio. On one side of this foyer is a guest bedroom with its private bathroom. The door to the kitchen is on the other side. There is another door also along this wall, mysterious to us as it has a steel triple-bolt lock. Curious what is beyond we release it. Well worn, uneven stone steps with a wiggly rope railing lead down to a cellar. Its walls are thick, and there is a stone bench built around three sides of the room. We understand bedding might be laid on these or kegs of wine could be stored for the temperature is quite cool. Originally this is where the wine for the villa was made and is called the cantina. There is only one small window, hardly sufficient for light. We are told this room may be used as a bomb shelter. That statement gives us pause. We Americans do not think in terms of needing bomb shelters even though most Europeans have such provisions in their homes.

Back up the stairs from the cantina and straight through the foyer into a wide passageway, the living room is on the right. Down two steps on the left of the same hallway is the dining room. The kitchen for the Poggio is behind the dining room. There is an outside door at the end of the dining room, opening onto the terrace and the courtyard of the driveway. The driveway has a gate, which is closed.

The living room is rectangle shaped. Its end wall, looking toward the garden is entirely glass, bulletproof glass, we are proudly told. This wall is a sliding door, which is huge and heavy and reaches from floor to ceiling. It opens outside directly onto the terrace with the rose garden through which Massimo had chased the cat. At the opposite end of the living room is a stone fireplace. It seems oversized for the room. The adjacent side wall has a door which opens out onto a loggia. There a ping-pong table is set up ready to use.

The loggia turns to the right following all the way to the front door. There is terracing to the gate by the road where we entered with our real estate agent. In warm weather these loggias would be wonderful for eating outside. There is a high fence entirely across the street side of the property. No one driving along via di Riboia can see into the lower part of the house or its grounds. This privacy is thoughtfully constructed because there is only a short distance from the house to the public road. One must ring a bell at the gate to enter. The gate is always locked.

A caretaker's apartment adjoins the main house. It is connected to it by a hallway through our communal laundry room, just beyond the Poggio's kitchen. The caretaker's home consists of two bedrooms and a combination kitchen-dining-sitting room.

Outdoors toward the right corner of the property in a lovely flowery setting is a swimming pool. It is not filled as the weather is too cold. A two car garage is built under the rose garden terrace, an ideal out-of-sight place. It was constructed underground as no other structure on the property was permitted by the authorities.

૯

The Tuscan officials never want properties changed and give renovators much hassle. Anything at all done construction-wise, simple or complicated, must be accounted for by written documentation to show to the inspectors. They check these statements with the work to be sure it matches, a painful process which is extremely annoying to the contractors and owners. The fact is the officials seldom allow anyone the necessary permits to do any construction. This is one reason why one sees so many buildings falling into ruin in the Tuscany region.

૯

The Poggio is owned by a young couple whose home is in Paris. His ancestry is French while she is of Norwegian heritage and born in the United States. Her family owns a villa nearby. They are the parents of four teenage children.

A young Italian husband and wife by the name of Sante and Dilia Casini and their son, Massimo, live at the Poggio the entire year. They are originally from the city of Grosseto. They are now employed as the Poggio's caretakers. Dilia is the housekeeper. While Sante has a full time job in town, he does yard and maintenance work on his time off. Dilia literally runs two homes. Her services are a part of our lease agreement.

❧

I am excited by the spaciousness and proportions of Poggio Ramerino and its surrounding grounds. The house is small and modest by Italian villa standards, but its appearance with its simple lines is clean and modern. Both house and yard have ample room. Care was taken in that planning I am sure. Some villas are immense. While hugeness may be atmospheric, I think it emphasizes useless space. The Poggio has contained space, giving us the secure feeling of being both snug yet capacious. This is a result of planning. Undoubtedly the architect and owners talked a lot about what they wished to achieve with the renovation. Their concern has resulted with the practical needs of the family and the aesthetics of the property combining in a harmonious way.

What an excellent example of collaboration between owners and architect.

❧

Before we finalize any lease arrangement there is currently a major problem in Italy which we need to face. It

22

must be taken seriously and reconciled satisfactorily for our own peace of mind. In our thinking, of all the things possible as concerns while living here, this would have been the last on our list. The problem is our own personal safety.

At this period of history there is a general social unrest among the population. It first was particularly noticeable in the universities. Now it has developed into a workers' rights revolution. Terrorist groups are meandering throughout the country, kidnapping and kneecapping not only prominent Italians, but oddly enough foreigners as well. Unhappily for us there does not seem to be any precise logic to which are more sought. Worse, the police are not in control of the situation. One group called the Red Brigade is especially notorious and absolutely terrifying everyone. They kidnapped, then assassinated Aldo Moro, the Christian Democrat Prime Minister in May 1978. His body was found in the trunk of a car. A heinous act! No one can explain satisfactorily why this occurred, nor have those responsible been found. There is no question tourism has been affected in this nervous atmosphere. Some members of our own family think we are foolish to consider a lease or even to be visiting Italy at this time.

Although these incidents had mostly taken place around major cities in the southern part of Italy, we would be unwise to disregard them here in northern Italy. We already had indication to be alert while sightseeing in Florence recently with Fred. That day he was driving a large Mercedes limousine. We were halted by some young Italian men who had blocked all traffic on the street. When we did pass by them, they looked and shook their fists at us. Who were we to go around their city in such a vehicle, they seemed to be saying. Italians are very vocal in expressing themselves. They exercise their voices in situations some Americans are apt to wield their fists. We were aware some Italians carry guns too so that day we hastened past without turning around to look at them.

℅

We learn most affluent Italians drive small, old cars for anonymity. Everybody dresses inconspicuously and wears jewelry of little value. People have learned through experience thieves watch for persons overdressed and over-jeweled and discover where they live either by following them or tracing their residences by the license plates on their automobiles. If they can get into their homes, they take whatever is there of value. That is thought of as sharing the wealth. Robbing a home is not considered so serious a crime. Needless to say people go to extreme measures to lock their houses—windows, doors, gates all included.

℅

We think we shall be secure at Poggio Ramerino. It is off the beaten track. Undoubtedly the wretchedness of via di Riboia is great protection. No smart terrorist would choose to drive his car on it. The car might get mired in the mud in a get-away. Expecting such questions (her other foreign clients were also concerned), our real estate agent has a prepared map showing choices of several entrances and exits to and from the neighborhood. In addition from checking the house we know it can be tightly secured. If absolutely necessary, we can always crawl into the bomb shelter!

We personally feel no sense of danger driving or walking anywhere, but we do realize we should always be alert for any unusual signs. Safety is a serious matter in Italy at this time.

With our main worry alleviated, we sign the lease. Poggio Ramerino will be home April, May and June of 1980. We can return now to the United States with plans firmly in place. There we shall daydream a lot about these lovely Italian surroundings, and before long it will be time to prepare for our return. We visualize a warm, balmy springtime where we shall leisurely enjoy sightseeing along with living at the Poggio and the challenge of learning a new language . . . Learning the language? That presents an interesting new problem: We need a teacher! Where will we find one?

Are we taking on more than we can handle—renting a house way out in the country in a foreign land where we do not know the language and have no American friends for support? Momentous decisions in the life of two newly retired. We both are elated and apprehensive!

A message awaits us when we arrive late March at the Excelsior Hotel. It is from the Poggio's owners and asks if we would ring them immediately. What has happened? We are troubled by this unexpected call immediately suspecting something has gone wrong with our lease.

The minute we settle in our room, Mac telephones. A most cordial voice greets him. They would like to meet us. Could we lunch together? At the Poggio, perhaps? Why not the day we move in and they leave for Paris? Good! Noon would be the perfect time. Mac hangs up obviously relieved. We are pleased with the invitation.

Once again we hire Frederick Hand to take us. He will return later that afternoon with our luggage. While happy to see us back in Italy, he voices misgivings about driving his clean, finely tuned car on muddy, bumpy via di Riboia. We tease him saying we will probably make it. He grins. We are off in high spirits!

♬

Turning onto via di Riboia, we see the entire surface has been newly paved. Astonishing! Someone once said an improved road loses all its character. Possibly true, but we welcome this smoothly graded black asphalt. It is such an improvement for the entire neighborhood. Even the apprehensive, usually glum Fred smiles. White curb markers are set on either side so no one can doubt where the asphalt stops. They look like smallish tombstones! We wonder aloud how long the markers will last, observing the driving habits of the natives.

♬

At the Poggio, we are warmly greeted by its owners and two of their four children. Since they are to begin the long journey to Paris, they suggest we all immediately assemble at the dining room table. We Americans and French get to know each other the Italian way—eating! We consume a delicious steak dinner with fresh vegetables from their garden, wine, and end with a huge dolce, a tasty sweet tart, for dessert. There is laughter and friendly conversation, everyone having a delightful time. (This is our first taste of Dilia's cooking. What a happy surprise!)

ଵ

While they finish last minute packing, we have a chance to walk around. The entire interior is changed! Not only is a lot of furniture attractively arranged, there are pictures hanging on walls, rugs on floors, all sorts of interesting arredi, knick-knacks, in various places, even bouquets of flowers here and there. It has a comfortable, lived-in appearance. Obviously the family enjoys their Italian home. Leaving it looking so pretty for us is a cheerful welcoming. We are touched by their concern for our happiness.

We had no inkling all these additional furnishings would be here. Independent souls that we are, who try to prepare in advance, we had made our own arrangements. No way did we wish to come for a stay of three months to find an uncomfortable villa—partially or maybe even totally unfurnished. Prior to leaving Florence after signing the lease, we worked out a floor plan, a scheme using new wicker furniture in the living room. Momentarily it is arriving by truck. How do we explain this to the family?

☙

"Oh, excuse me, Mr. Whiting," says la Signora coming into the living room, where we are sitting, trying to be out of everybody's way. "I wonder if I can ask a favor of you?"

"Why, of course," replies Mac, standing to greet her. "What may we do?"

"I have two lamps being repaired in Florence which are suppose to be on those end tables either side of the fireplace. They were not ready for your arrival, I am sorry to say, but they will be finished before you leave. Do you suppose it would be too much out of your way to pick them up for me?"

"We would be happy to do that. Where is the shop and how do we identify them?" asks Mac.

"Here is a card with the address of the shop. It is in the via Maggio district. Do you think you can find it without too much trouble?

"I'm sure we can," answers Mac.

"So you will recognize them, the lamps are carved and gilded, three-footed with parchment shades—about this tall." She shows their height with her hands. "I will telephone the shop's owner that you will be coming for them," she adds.

"Don't worry we shall be happy to get them for you," replies Mac for us both.

"Thank you so much. I do appreciate it," she smiles.

☙

They are ready to leave. Baggage, boxes, and loose

clothing are tossed into the trunk while everybody loudly proclaims where they wish to sit in the car. That discussion is important since the car will be jammed with people. A last item to cope with is a huge mirror with an elaborately carved, golden gilt frame. With much commotion it is strapped to the roof of the car. We watch the procedure wondering if it will make the trip unbroken! Finally everything is assembled. People climb inside, and car doors slam shut. Arms wildly waving goodbye out of all the windows and shouting uproariously "luck and happiness" to us, they are off. Our last glimpse is a mahogany-colored Citroen, its chassis hunkered down low on the tires, turning out the driveway. Every corner is stuffed, and the well-roped mirror lies serenely tied on the roof!

No sooner has the Citroen disappeared down via di Riboia than we see a Mercedes and a pickup truck come up the opposite direction. What perfect timing! Fred with our luggage is leading a truck filled with wicker furniture. The truck has so many pieces it is bulging on all sides. Fred is driving very slowly so the truck can follow with nothing toppling off. Quickly Mac and I run back into the house calling Dilia to help. We must remove the owners' things from the living room. Totally non-plussed she suggests storing them in a little closed-off room between the living and dining rooms. Since it is unfinished, needing lighting fixtures as well as furnishings, this room is a perfect storage space. It might have been an ideal study or library.

31

Mac asks the men to bring in the pieces. At our request the store sent a large assortment so we can make an on-site selection. Of the many styles available we could not tell in the store which would look best in the house. There are choices of small sofas, tables, benches, chairs and a chest or two. Florentines are very accommodating merchants.

𝕮

We begin by establishing a seating arrangement around the fireplace, the logical spot for group sitting. We use two small sofas and various glass-topped tables. When la Signora's lamps are finished, they will light this end of the living room perfectly. It looks most inviting. To balance this, at the other end of the room, we choose a large, tall table with a round glass top. This will display magazines and flower arrangements beautifully. We place a low cabinet against the side wall which opens onto the loggia. We shall use it as a bar. (The actual bar is a small room at a right angle to the sliding door. Hidden behind a curtain, we did not immediately see it. It is only partially finished with no cabinets or piping for the sink and refrigerator.) Finally, we position two large square benches in front of the sliding door. They will be fun for sitting and leisurely enjoying the views of the countryside. Such a dominant feature in the room, this huge sliding door with its bullet-proof glass!

𝕮

Freed of the clutter of heavy upholstered furniture, the whole room becomes spacious and airy. We can sit almost anywhere and enjoy the wondrous vistas of the outside. We like that fresh openness. When filling a room with furniture, we know it critical to remember the use of space is as important as furniture. We think we have achieved that balance.

One last look-about: A rug in front of the fireplace between the new seating arrangement would soften the area. We try the owners' colorful oriental. This is the missing link which ties everything together. Pleased with the results of our efforts we scan the room to see if we need any more wicker furniture. Everything seems perfect so we thank the delivery men and tell them to repack the rest to go back to the store.

᭡

Dilia industriously helps us with this rearranging. We worry she may be insulted when we displace her things with these wicker pieces. On the contrary she is most enthusiastic. She walks around, smiling, saying, "Bene! Molto bene!!" "Nice! Very nice!!" She has never been involved in organizing a furniture arrangement of this scope. It is not a part of her duties, but she thoroughly enjoys participating.

᭡

Fred is standing about, slightly bored, yawning once or twice and smoking a good bit. Occasionally he helps move a chair or two. He is patiently waiting to unpack his car. Forgetting this in our excitement, we decide a cup of espresso would be most welcome. Fred guesses he could do with one too. Dilia, happy to do something in the kitchen, bounces out. Nothing so soothes tired backs and sore muscles as an Italian espresso. We spoon generous teaspoonfuls of sugar into our cups, savor its aroma, then enjoy the bitter smoothness of Dilia's delicious brew. Good espresso like this leaves a taste in one's mouth similar to dark, rich chocolate.

Finishing their last sip Fred and Mac go to Fred's car and start carrying in our belongings among which are three paintings. They hand them to me. I unwrap, look at them and blink in disbelief.

"Mac! Come see." Pointing to our pictures, I exclaim, "Isn't this hilarious, but disappointing! They're just pathetic and forlorn in this room. What's wrong? We can't possibly hang them here, can we?"

"No, we absolutely cannot," he replies. "They're certainly colorful, but they're not strong enough." Mac and I laugh as we study them. "Its their frames more than anything, don't you think?" we say almost in unison.

Our modern paintings are no great works of art, but with their clean, steel frames are so totally understated, they are completely diminished in this environment. If we hang them, they simply must be redone with Italian framing. All of us, including Fred and Dilia, who had come in to see what is the commotion, burst out laughing.

34

ế

When an Italian frames a picture it is done with lavishness, none of this Yankee modern austerity for them. It makes no difference whether the composition inside is good or bad. The frame is as important as the picture, and perhaps, sometimes more. They adore ornateness with much carving of flowers and leaves, sometimes also little putti, which when originally done in the fifteenth century, were representations of chubby children. Always there is lots of gilt. What is interesting is this flim-flam complements the Italian space in which they are hung. Our poor paintings looked undernourished! No question about it, the owners' great grandfather, a not too expertly painted portrait, but most opulent in its baroque frame, will stay on the wall. Its rococesque quality blends perfectly in this living room's atmosphere.

With a flourish we hustle ours off to the study / storage room. They will stay there until we can return them to the United States. Little do we suspect the trouble this will cause.

ế

Finished! We stand back and scrutinize our work. The ambiance seems right. Oh . . . in dashes Dilia, interrupting thoughts . . . with a pretty bouquet of wild flowers! She places it on the tall, large table with the round glass top. The perfect final touch. How wonderful of her to volunteer this. The room is now ready to use. It has been worth the time and effort organizing it. We thank both Fred and Dilia for their help . . .

Good heavens, the time! Fred must go. We have been so preoccupied we did not realize how much time has slipped by. Now it is later than we promised to keep him. Mac thanks Fred for his generosity and apologizes for detaining him. We walk with him to his car, saying we shall be watching for a limousine with an English driver when we are in Florence. With a buss on either cheek for me, (he always greets me this way no matter whether we have just arrived or are about to depart!) and a handshake for Mac, he is off.

§

The fresh air feels so good! We take several deep gulps and stretch, and twist, and stretch again. We are refreshed to muster up strength and enthusiasm to unpack our clothing. Up the stairs to the bedroom, and immediately a problem arises. Oh, who has energy to solve a problem? Any problem. The pole in my clothes closet is so high I cannot begin to touch it. Help! Dove lo sgabello? Or some other doohickey to stand on so I can reach the rod. Those tall, tall Poggio owners. They never anticipated a tiny little renter like me.

M ac hears of an excellent language teacher by the name of Giovanna Fenyes. She is recommended by a business friend of his, whose daughter had worked at the United States Consulate in Florence and knew Giovanna's husband. Adalberto is still an employee. By calling him at the Consulate, we may learn how to reach her. Mac telephones. Would she have lunch and talk about teaching us Italian? Indeed, it would be her pleasure!

We are a bit apprehensive about the meeting, not knowing what to expect an Italian language teacher might be like. We are seated in a hotel dining room waiting for her. The minute she appears at the entrance, we recognize Giovanna as our person. She has a huge smile on her face, making her olive brown eyes crinkly and friendly. Her hair is auburn colored with an excellent short haircut which curls softly around her face and shines with highlights. Her skin is the golden color typical of so many Tuscans. She is medium size and is loaded down with a bulging tote bag on one arm and a puffed-out purse in the other.

🙢

Introducing herself, she manages to shake hands with us both without dropping her gear. We smile and invite her to sit down. The tote and purse disappear under the table. Menus are offered. We ask her what she prefers to eat at lunch time, a sandwich or something more substantial. She announces since this is her big meal of the day, and if we do not mind, she will order the steak. Do we know that Florentine steak is very good? We tell her we understand it is excellent and please order it. We, however, are small lunch eaters and does she mind if we eat a salad with a little cheese? That's fine with her. Do we care if she smokes? Such a terrible habit, so bad for one's health, she sighs, lighting the cigarette, but she just loves to smoke.

🙢

With this as our introduction, Giovanna turns to me and says, "Now, Mrs. Whiting, let me hear you say the vowels."

"A, E, I, O, U," I utter quickly.

"No, no, Mrs. Whiting, I mean in Italian!"

"I don't know how in Italian, Mrs. Fenyes."

"Look at me, Mrs. Whiting. This is how they sound, and please, call me Giovanna. She articulates each vowel, deliberately puckering her lips to make more emphatic the sound.

"Now, you—Mr. Whiting . . . Ah, that's better. Let me hear you say U. Very good! You have studied language before?"

*

The food is served. Giovanna picks up her fork and knife and cuts into her steak with gusto.

Professionally she is a language teacher at the branch of Gonzaga University in Florence. Her pupils are mostly foreigners and beginning language students. Additionally she often has classes for the wives of the officials at the Consulate plus she does some tutoring of private students at her home. She is educated in Italy and earned a scholarship to a southern college in the United States. It was there she perfected her English. She is proud to be Tuscan-born and tells us of the many Italian dialects, Tuscan is the purest—the only one to spend time learning.

*

During the rest of the luncheon we discuss plans for our lessons. She proposes we work at her home every afternoon Monday through Friday from about one thirty until six or six thirty. She makes clear that while this is a crash course, she teaches academic Italian. Berlitz-style is not her method. She will cover the text as quickly as we are able. She wants us to know, however, the amount of work she proposes covering, she usually teaches in one semester. We have not given her that much time. She intends to concentrate on correct pronunciation and grammar. We will read aloud, have conversations and write. She states she gives daily assignments and expects this homework ready to be checked by her the next day. She stresses again there is much material to cover in the time we are allotting. Are we willing to study this hard?

Mac brightens and says it sounds just wonderful to him. He can speak French and some German. I scowl and think this sounds difficult. My previous language experience was studying Latin and a bit of French. I have never really experienced the repartee of a language other than English. I am not sure how to go about learning a spoken language. "Well, why not try?" I say to myself. "I'm game." Mac and Giovanna decide classes should start immediately. She seems like an ideal person to teach both of us. She speaks excellent English and a beautiful melodious Italian.

Once we start, the lessons shape up our day. Every morning we breakfast at eight. Afterwards we separate, finding individual quiet spots to do homework. There is vocabulary to learn, sentences to write, and paragraphs to translate. Usually there is some verb, indubitably an irregular one, which Giovanna wants us to learn with all its tenses. Soon it seems to me all Italian verbs are irregular! When everything is completed the entire morning is gone.

𝄢

I am shocked to realize just how much time we are going to devote assimilating this language. It will be our major project. This is acceptable to us. We would rather be doing something like this than constantly entertaining or being entertained or art researching or simply dawdling. We will be studying with textbook seven or eight hours a day. That is thirty-five to forty hours per week! It breaks down to four hours in the morning doing the homework, then four hours in the afternoon with Giovanna. That is a lot of concentration on one subject. While we need this total immersion to help us hear and learn quickly, we soon find the process is exhausting. Our brains can absorb only so much. By bedtime our tongues feel thick and weary. Whoever would guess one's tongue, unaccustomed to pronouncing another language, would need rest? It is a total revelation to this person who never remembers needing a rest from talking! To help keep perspective, we decide each weekend to go on overnight excursions to various areas within driving distance of the Poggio. That should help clear the mental cobwebs.

𝄢

One morning I must take a break from homework. I go exploring around the Poggio and discover a room, a sort of private hide-a-way. I immediately appropriate it as mine, and mine alone. It is exactly the kind of spot I enjoy working in to be away from the hustle-bustle of the household.

The hide-a-way is at the top of the staircase from our dressing room. It is the interior of the tower of the Poggio. Small and square shaped with a high ceiling, there are big windows on three walls, and a pigeon roost constructed on the fourth, facing the road. With the exception of a single bed by the staircase, and a card table and chair folded against a wall, there is no other furniture in the room. The pigeon roost has six nesting houses, each with a tiny flat floor and rounded, dome-shaped top, all adjacent to each other. While this is picturesque, I am thankful the entire roost is covered by glass on the inside. Pigeon cooing could be distracting, although they might be fun to watch. Now there are no birds. I wonder if any will make nests while we live here.

I place the card table and chair so when sitting, I look at via di Riboia through the window ahead, then turning a hundred and eighty degrees, down the road through the window behind. To my left are the two other windows which show the blurry outlines of Florence in the far away distance. What fun to have a place like this to use! It is the perfect quiet spot. Being high up gives new perspective to the gentle, rolling land around the Poggio. It looks quite beautiful. I shall sit at the small table with typewriter humming and be inspired to tell our adventures. This is my Pigeon's Roost.

☙

"Tutto Firenze!" says Dilia, pointing out the front windows of the Pigeon's Roost. She has come up to see what I am doing and/or if I need anything. She is pleased I am finding this little room useful. She realizes I am not to be disturbed when I am here. She is merely checking, I am not!

☙

Promptly at noon homework stops, and Dilia serves lunch. How welcome that is. We are starved. What appetites after smelling her cooking all morning. We remind her we want a small meal. If we eat too much, we shall fall asleep in our lesson with Giovanna.

The drive to Giovanna's home will take about a half hour, depending on the amount of traffic. To reach her we drive through the center of Florence. This can be a muddle of cars, trucks, mo-peds and people—intricate maneuvering for Mac and unnerving for us both.

Her street is called Carnesecche. Translated this means dry meat. We have a good laugh over the absurdity of a street called dry meat.

☙

Driving through the city to her apartment everybody on the road is hurrying, weaving their vehicle in and out of the traffic which seems to come from all directions simultaneously. There is never any set pattern to its flow, other than everybody trying to be first: first to turn, first to start when the light changes, first to pass a car. Either side will do.

⚡

We arrive at Giovanna's with frazzled nerves. We ring her bell. She replies by buzzing the door opener, which allows us to enter the foyer of the building. We proceed to walk up to her apartment which is on the top floor. This exercise relaxes us. It horrifies Giovanna. Why not use the elevator? No one walks when there is an elevator. Since she is a heavy smoker, her lung power is shallow, and climbing is torture. She cannot imagine anyone voluntarily doing that for enjoyment or for any other reason.

⚡

Up we go, floor by floor. As we pass each apartment doorway, I read the nameplate saying, "Buon giorno, Signora Luciano, buon giorno, Signora Lucini, Signora Fantechi, Signora Squanci," . . . on and on until we reach the top floor. Looking up as we climb, there is Giovanna, leaning over the railing, laughing.

"Buon giorno!" she says in her low, friendly voice.

44

"Buon giorno, Signora Giovanna Cini Corsini Fenyes," I answer, reading her nameplate.

"Come in," chuckles Giovanna. "Please come in. Our home is your home. Prego!"

We go into her living room and sit down in opposite chairs with Giovanna on the sofa between us. Usually the conversation starts with one of us saying, "Giovanna, you won't believe what happened . . ." Maybe it was in Florence, or in our neighborhood, whatever. There is almost always some little incident that has tickled our ribs yesterday or the day before. Leaning forward to concentrate on the speaker, Giovanna says, "Tell me about it." We sit there retelling the story. Giovanna, who has the greatest sense of humor in the world, starts to chuckle, her eyes wrinkle, and her whole body shakes with laughter. We laugh too, sometimes so hard tears form in our eyes. All of us totally relax. Then, "Aspetta!" Giovanna is saying it is time to go to work. Taking a big gulp of air, we dig into the lesson.

Many times I look forward to these storytelling sessions more than the lesson. We three are developing a mutual congeniality that makes a friendly student-teacher relationship.

Our work stops only once during the afternoon. That is

45

for a coffee break. Giovanna makes espresso, the only culinary achievement she claims to do well. She serves it in tiny cups and adores her own double portion with a heaping spoonful of sugar, and always, her cigarette. Such a chain smoker she is, promising to give up the bad habit each time she has one. The coffee is delicious and relaxes us, although our stomachs cannot tolerate double portions of the potent stuff. Sometimes we eat a caramella, a fruit-flavored hard candy, too.

⌇

The lesson ends when Alberto comes home. This may be six, six thirty or even seven o'clock. He, their son, Didi, and daughter, Mimma, join us in the living room. We chat a bit before leaving. The somewhat formal Alberto, his correct name is Adalberto, but always is called Alberto, shakes hands with Mac. He bows and kisses mine. Didi, the shiest Fenyes and not comfortable speaking English, bows formally to both of us. Mimma smiles and waves. She often has long conversations with us during our afternoon coffee break, speaking excellent English. She adores learning American slang. We told her she should not use the word "ain't" even if her Irish nun teacher says it is proper. She is a bubbly, blue-eyed blonde who is at ease with everyone. Strangely, she is the one Giovanna worries about most. We think she seems the most secure of them all.

⌇

(Interesting to me: I observe Alberto has steel blue eyes while Giovanna's are a greenish brown. Didi is dark, almost black eyed, while Mimma is entirely blue eyed. Strange how genes work in one family.)

🜚

The two Fenyes children are formally named Sigfried and Arabella, but everybody calls them Didi and Mimma. When we first meet them, Didi is a university student, and Mimma is finishing high school. It is soon apparent they are being brought up very differently. The girl, we are told, is having a hard time with her lessons, but hopefully she will graduate. "We keep our fingers crossed," says her mother. The boy studies two majors, law, jurisprudence Giovanna calls it, and orchestra conducting, which involves mastering the piano. Both are demanding courses, but, when in time he finishes, he will have a career choice. "Of course, we have to sacrifice for these children," she adds.

🜚

Unlike his sister, Didi is reserved and serious. He teaches piano lessons to a couple of young boys. He says they are not good students because they will not practice—that is, not enough to satisfy the perfectionist Didi. Weekends he is on call with the volunteer ambulance corps. Like all Italian young men he is eligible for a year of military service. Fenyes' hope this may be postponed until he has completed his

47

schooling, although this is unlikely. Now most of his time is devoted to his studies. He works in his bedroom, which has two pianos, plus his bed and desk. This room has been wood paneled to soundproof it because the neighbors complained about his piano practicing being too loud. The paneling was a serious expense for the Fenyes, but necessary, they felt, for Didi's career. In contrast Mimma finally has a bedroom to herself. She had shared it with her Grandmother until her Grandmother's recent death. The room is nice, but not the size of her brother's. She spends an enormous amount of time there alone studying.

$$\mathcal{C}$$

We quiz Didi about his law course. It involves some class participation, but it is mostly individualistic study. He works several months reading on his own, and mostly at home, for an oral examination. When he passes the exam, he goes onto the next section. This procedure continues until he has finished the entire law course. There is little, if any, actual lecturing by the professors.

One recent oral exam he took incensed him. The professor asked a question requiring some original interpretation from the text Didi had been studying. Didi thought this unfair. He thinks an exam question should be based only on the material as written in the text. That is what he has learned and how he expects to answer. Interpretation is an unknown quality, something he has not been taught. Asking him to do this during an examination made him uncomfortable and uncertain. He had been doing well on his exams. This time he did not. He was morally indignant, because he felt it was not his fault. The professor had treated him unfairly.

In Italy the law derives from a written code and not from a loosely structured sequence of judicial decisions as in our laws. Italian law sits above and remote from world experience.

It is not customary for an Italian law student to clerk in a firm while still a student. Their counterparts in the United States do this as a part of their learning. Usually the American students seek work in the second year of law school. Ideally they would like a job in a firm where they might establish themselves as future lawyers. By working summers, or whatever time they have available away from their formal studies, gives them a taste of practical law and also helps pay their tuition. In contrast no one would dream of hiring a student to do this in Italy. Italian law students are merely bookworms at this stage of their careers. It is a wonder they do not become discouraged and give up. With so much solitary studying the goal of actually reaching a bread-and-butter job undoubtedly must seem a long way off. Hopefully this goal is not forgotten.

❧

An epilogue to every lesson was our drive back to the Poggio. We go down to our car which sits half on the sidewalk and half on the street for lack of parking space. (All Italians park their cars haphazardly, especially when space is at a premium, and they are in a hurry.) We get in, fasten our seatbelts and head toward the stadium. There we turn right past the bar and social club of the Violets, the soccer team of Florence. As we proceed around the stadium, we go by the open ground where there is usually a carnival or gypsy encampment of some kind. We pass the popular ice cream stand which usually has a line of waiting customers. Several blocks along we come to the ring road, built on the site of the old wall of the city. The wall was torn down about a century ago. It is now a boulevard which goes all the way around the city. Here we encounter our first real traffic—a mix of bicycles, mo-peds, three-wheeled trucks, mini cars, normal size cars, delivery vans—all dashing to be first. Reaching the destination safely is incidental to the aims of beating the adjacent car—in the most blase sort of way, of course. We come to the railroad overpass where three lines of traffic become two very tight ones. The expected major pile-up never happens although we certainly do not know why. A half mile further on we run into the river. We are not allowed to turn left as we need to, but must go right for a quarter mile. We then turn away from the river, turn again in the wrong direction, turn one more time to head back toward the river, and now reaching the river the traffic is one-way with four lanes all heading in the direction we want to go. Into this

50

stream we must fight our way. We come to the bridge across the Arno, only a mere two blocks from where we made all this elaborate turning!

On the other side of the river traffic is very light. We can often go eighty kilometers per hour as we race toward the center of town. By now I am ashen, and Mac has ceased swearing. At the end of this straight-away lies the jam at the south end of the Ponte Vecchio. Here there is a single line of traffic in either direction with hoards of pedestrians wending their way through it. No one gets hit! A little further on we stop for a newspaper. Since there is no defined parking area, Mac stops the car in any vacant spot, leaving the motor running and dashes out of the car to pick up today's copy of the *International Herald Tribune.* I sit, biting my fingernails, certain the car will be hit or the police will ticket us. Neither ever happens. The obstructed traffic seldom gets very upset for surely someone else has done something more outrageous. We continue on down a maze of one-way streets and after several more turns we reach the Porta Romana. Here six roads intersect. The car going into the intersection has the right-of-way. Every night we manage to get through without a scrape.

From there on it is a mere fifteen minutes of driving through twisty country lanes to reach the Poggio. Once there we take a moment to enjoy the quietness and peace of our garden. We are ready for a shower before Dilia announces dinner.

Dilia is a young, energetic, happy woman in her early thirties. She is short, not even five feet, stocky, full-busted, with dark black hair, rosy red cheeks and black sparkling eyes. Every day she dresses in a freshly laundered blue jean skirt and a red, short-sleeved t-shirt. She wears backless shoes, a Dr. Scholl-type, with medium high wooden heels, giving her a little more height. They make a great clatter as she walks on our stone floors, but we always know where she is! Besides cooking she washes and irons and cleans until everything in the entire house is spotless and shining. Dilia is an immaculate, proud housekeeper. Knowing we enjoy fresh flowers and without asking, she keeps arrangements of fiori di campo in every room including our bathroom. These are the wild flowers which grow in the fields around the Poggio. Sometimes picking them is a bit hazardous. Although there are signs posted saying, divieto di caccia, meaning no hunting, BeBe guns frequently are heard. Small birds like thrush are much sought by hunters as delicacies to eat . . . Dilia never has enough flower vases so she uses anything handy, be that a coffee can, or a jam jar. The best vase of all is a ceramic duck! She sweeps out and sets the fireplace each morning, using olive tree prunings as apparently there is no other firewood available. She serves our meals. She does all this for us as well as looking after Massimo, Sante and their apartment. Watching the energetic Massimo is a full time task in itself. He is not too obedient, a great tease, and plenty noisy.

Wonderful as it is, living at Poggio Ramerino is not quite like having a room at a hotel where a button can be pushed for service. There you feel in charge. Here we should be and are not. We are keeping house with our own housekeeper, only we cannot ask her for the simplest things. She only speaks Italian while we only speak English. This makes communication a difficult challenge, and it is frustrating for she does not want us to do anything for ourselves. If we want something like a glass of water, for instance, we pantomime this is what we wish. We do try some Italian while she tries some English. All of us talk and gesture and pretend to understand each other while none of us really do. This makes us feel in limbo. Thank goodness for the relaxed sense of humor we three have or life might be a bit grim. It is essential for us to understand Italian. It is back to basics to learn all those words we take for granted in English. This is a rather sobering experience at our age.

On our first morning we elect to eat breakfast in the kitchen where it is cozy and warm. As we start to converse with her, Dilia shakes her head, saying, "un momento!" She leaves the room and returns with a huge Italian/English dictionary, which she proudly hands to us. That beautiful dizionario is a gift to her from the owners of the Poggio. How it saves our lives! We henceforth refer to it as italiano/inglese. As we eat, the three of us communicate. Using the English side for us and the Italian side for her, and many hand gestures to emphasize, we plan our meals. Without its help I am not sure what we might have been fed. At the same time we are entertained by radio music, lively early morning jazz from Radio Monte Carlo. From now on each morning will begin like this. It's a spirited start to our day.

Breakfast for me is tea and toast. For Mac it is cereal with cream, toast and coffee. Dilia cuts the bread for the toast as we wait. She holds the loaf close to her chest and slices toward her body with a big broad knife. These slices invariably burn in the toaster, but taste reasonably good. For some reason Mac's cereal cream, a brand called Parmalat, does not pour from its foil-lined container. Mac must unlump it with a spoon before he can use it on his cereal. Asked whether it is sour, he assures me it is fresh and good tasting, but each morning the same thing occurs. We never understand why. Dilia sees him stirring furiously, but apparently does not find this unusual. We do not begin to know the Italian words to ask her why it is lumpy. She never has it unlumped before we sit down. After several similar mornings we cannot look at each other while he performs the unlumping ritual. It seems very funny. We do not want to insult Dilia's food by laughing out loud. Why she buys this particular brand, we cannot figure out.

〰

Dilia never thinks we have enough to eat. We constantly say "no, no, Dilia—too much." We finally learn the word basta which means enough and that helps solve the arguments. All our meals are planned around whatever is currently fresh at the market. Mac says he will eat most anything she prepares because it is so good, except rabbit. He can not stand rabbit, coniglio. Every so often Dilia with a twinkle in her eye will propose coniglio for dinner, knowing full well she will get a great reaction. We all laugh until tears come to our eyes.

〰

Dilia's grocery store is no U.S.A. supermarket type. It is a tiny, little hole-in-the-wall about a mile from us in Pozzolatico. Each day after our breakfast discussion, Dilia telephones her order. Later they deliver the food to our door in their three-wheeled mini-truck. Everything they sell is fresh that morning whether it is vegetables or fruit, picked from a garden, eggs newly lain, bread, baked that morning in the bakery close by, or meat, just butchered. We thrive on these fresh foods. Our posta, post office, is in Pozzolatico too, another little hole-in-the-wall. When a letter came to us from our daughter-in-law, Sara, it was ceremoniously delivered to our door by the mailman from that posta.

We are impressed with these friendly services in our new neighborhood.

Several weeks later, when some of our children visited, they jogged each morning. One farm they passed had two baby goats. Knowing Dilia's and their parents' fondness for fresh food, they were paralyzed the baby goats might end up on the dinner table! (Need I add, they never did?)

While we always had delicious milk to drink, it suddenly occurs to us we never see cows during our meanderings through the countryside. There are lots of sheep and goats, but not one cow. That begins to bother us so we asked

57

Giovanna a little later on, if there really are cows in Italy, not that we are so fond of cows, but our milk was coming from somewhere not apparent.

"Certamente," she replies, a little put out with such a ridiculous, non-language question. She is correcting our homework, which is important.

"But where are they?" we persist. "Oh, in the mountains around Bologna and Milan," she answers with a wave of her hand.

Now we know. We will be on the lookout for them, but we are reassured our milk is from a cow, not some other four-legged critter, a fact we did not want to explain to Giovanna.

Later on we finally saw cows grazing. En route from Porto Ercole to Siena are lovely rolling fields and valleys for miles and miles. In that green grass we saw a sizable herd of Guernseys. They were obviously contented.

We notice signs along the highway with pictures of cattle. If one comes onto the highway, the driver has fair warning to be aware. Why would any cow leave these lush, green fields—ever?

Another herd we happened upon had impressive long horns which stood straight up from their heads. Giovanna said these are a special breed of cattle raised for beef. They are called Razza Chianina, from the Chianti zone. The best Florentine beef served in restaurants are from these cattle. She stated they are not too prevalent anymore because so many were bought and exported to Texas. Texas in the United States? Really!

We later learn it is more common practice for Italians to keep their cows inside barns. It is felt they spoil the fields when they wander around to graze. The farmer cuts and carries fodder to them. This is why one hardly ever sees any in the fields.

So much for our concern about things bovine. We learned more information than we truly wanted to know!

※

We never did find out why our Parmalat is always lumpy!

※

This spring of 1980 has the coldest temperatures for the season ever recorded in Italy. There is a new law stating all furnaces must be turned off on the fifteenth of April. This applies to private dwellings as well as public ones. An oil shortage crisis is in effect, and a national effort at fuel savings for energy conservation is taking place.

We are uncomfortable inside the house, and it is getting colder outside. We wonder if Dilia will follow the law to the letter and keep our furnace unlighted. The Poggio, after all, is a private home. We soon find out: She would, and she does!

Our furnace is off. Not one speck of warmth comes from any radiator in the entire house. We feel them all.

⟢

Mac and I, dressed in our cottons for the warm weather we expected, are colder by the hour. What an unpleasant dilemma! We do not know enough Italian to tell Dilia why she should turn on the furnace. Since we have just started our lease, we do not want to provoke unpleasantness by always complaining about being cold. Taking matters into our own hands, we drive into Florence and buy heavy sweaters. Most stores had put them away for fall weather so we are lucky to find any at all. More importantly we also buy an electric heater. Italians call it a stufa elettrica. This stufa we install in the small sitting room off the master bedroom. We turn it on and let it run all day and night. Using this and wearing our new sweaters, we feel a little more comfortable. Perhaps we should have a twinge of guilt about the amount of electricity we are using. It is too pleasant to be warm to worry about being patriotic.

When Dilia comes in the room to clean, she flaps her arms and pants, "caldo! caldo!!" She is letting us know she thinks the room is hot. She is too polite to turn the stufa off, but it is obvious she wishes we would.

⟢

Nothing is discussed between Dilia and ourselves about

fuel saving or energy conservation. These concerns are much too complicated to communicate. Perhaps we should contact our real estate agent to discuss the problem. (She had not offered help with any problem that might arise so we hesitate calling her. There is no one else we know to consult.) Never once does Dilia turn the furnace on even though she begins to realize we are uncomfortable. Mac and I keep believing the weather will change. Everybody tells us Italian springtimes are balmy and warm. We expect they are, and this one will be soon. The stores are full of lightweight clothing. Hopefully this is a good sign.

What a challenge to bathe each evening. We do so with great alacrity!

After breakfast Dilia's morning housekeeping begins. She opens all the windows in the entire Poggio. She wants the clean, fresh morning air to come into each room. The Poggio is already so cold one can hardly sit comfortably anywhere, and this keeps the place in a constant state of being really chilly.

She goes first to our bedroom. As the nice fresh air blows through the room, Dilia strips the bed and hangs this bedding outside from the window sill. The sheets and blankets will freshen in the morning breeze. She sweeps the floor, moving all the furniture, and thoroughly dusts every piece. She leaves the room with the windows open so everything can air completely a good half hour or more. Several times she shouts out of the window, "Massimo?

61

Where are you?" And Massimo shouts something back to her. That breaks our studying concentration for sure!

After a suitable length of time, which is usually long enough for all the nice fresh air to creep under the crack of the door, allowing adjoining rooms to cool off too, Dilia returns. The bedding is pulled inside, and the bed is remade. The furniture is rearranged in its proper positions. The rugs are replaced on the floor.

When everything is clean and shiny, Dilia closes the windows and pulls the shutters over them. The room is in total darkness. She leaves it this way. We never understand why a clean room is left in total darkness. Hotel maids do this too. Apparently it is the custom.

❦

"Yesterday or before yesterday, never in China!" sings Dilia with a big smile as she goes about her housework.

❦

The windows of the Poggio are elaborately designed. The casings are of wood which is placed in a stone frame. The glass of the window is set in the wooden frame. Over the glass is a wooden door which can be opened on its own hinge without opening the glass window. It can also be left closed while still opening the glass window.

Once the glass window is open an outside shutter can be pulled over an opening. At the Poggio the outer shutter is louvered and painted brown. We have two types of outside shutters—one type rolls up into the side wall of the house; the other type is a two shutter variety which swings outward and lies flat along the wall of the house. To open these shutters, which are used daily, a hinge latch must be turned forty five degrees. These hinges are often sticky and difficult to maneuver.

⅚

Architecturally windows are important. It is possible to determine the age of a villa by its windows. They make the style authentic.

⅚

The little boy peeks in at me. I am sitting at a desk in one of the upstairs bedrooms looking at my new electric typewriter. In Italian it is called a macchina da scrivere. It has a European keyboard which is not similar to an American typewriter keyboard. I am fascinated and trying to familiarize myself with its differences. I start to position my hands to type on it for the first time. Instead, I turn around to my visitor and say, "Hi! What's your name?"

He blinks, giggles, and yells, "Massimo!" Quickly he disappears around the corner. His mother has told him not to bother us. I turn on the machine and adjust the paper in the roller. Massimo is back, quietly tiptoeing into the room. I pay no attention, concentrating on making the typewriter work. All of a sudden the aroma of Wrigley's Juicy Fruit chewing gum seems to be surrounding me. Massimo, chomping away, is beside my right shoulder, not saying a word. I pretend I do not know he is there and begin typing. I write, "There is a little boy standing beside me. He is chewing gum. His name is Massimo."

A chubby finger suddenly shoots over my shoulder onto the paper, pointing to a word. "Massimo!" he loudly shouts in my ear and turns running out of the room.

I laugh aloud and think to myself, "Well, well! He can read his own name! That's pretty good at age four." A new thought comes to my mind. Remembering the pruning shears episode a few months ago, I say to myself, "I wonder whatever happened to that cat?"

From then on when anything at all happens involving Mac or I, be that something as simple as walking down the stairs, or going outside, or sitting in the living room by the fire before dinner, Massimo's curiosity about il Signore and la Signora gets the better of him. He has to see what we are doing. Wherever we are, he careens in, making a loud vocal noise at the same time. Careening means running at full tilt directly towards whatever object he chooses—us, a chair, a tree, whatever—stopping with a thump of his two feet mere inches away. Then he turns around and runs full speed back from where he came. One never knows from which direction or when he may appear. It is funny, but a bit disconcerting. At least we can hear him coming. This is a lot better than having him quietly peek at us around some corner. Dilia does not approve of such shenanigans. Massimo knows this and does it anyhow. We are not helping her by laughing. We think he is funny, and all Italian children are expected to be noisy and assertive. It is nice to have a young one around.

☙

Suddenly we begin to grasp some Italian. Three simple little words catch our ear. They are: ma ma, arrivederci, and ciao. Ma ma translates but but or maybe yes, maybe no; arrivederci means goodbye or 'til we meet again. Ciao is the least formal of the three. It means hi or bye bye or so long. One way or another these words seem to be used in most conversations.

It is a tiny beginning, but it is a glorious feeling to comprehend just a bit. We live in an all Italian neighborhood. Except for us, as far as we can ascertain, no one within miles speaks any English at all.

On the day of our first lesson Giovanna hands us a single textbook, "Parlo Italiano" by Luisa Rapaccini.

"I did not know whether to buy one book or two," she says and adds, "textbooks are quite expensive, you know."

"Giovanna, since we both are taking the lessons, how can we work with only one textbook?" we say in surprise. Neither Mac nor I wish to share. We have quite different studying habits.

"Well," replies Giovanna, thinking hard how to solve a major problem, yet please both of us, "Mr. Whiting, take the book, and Mrs. Whiting, you can have this pad and make notes as we go along. I will order another textbook, but it will be a while before it gets here."

𝕰

So I begin Italian the way our Grandson Mac is learning to write English by sounding it out phonetically. With an ear not trained in language sounds, my spelling is horrendous! Once I do hear Italian properly, the spelling is quite easy— more so than English. In the beginning, however, I never see the words I am trying to write. "This will certainly make reading a challenge, once I get that book!" I think to myself.

𝕰

This is my first experience with the phenomena I call masculine preferred. It starts innocently enough with an Italian grammar rule, but its concept seeps into the subconsciousness of the people. The rule, masculine preferred, means should there be a choice of which gender a word might be, masculine or feminine, the masculine will always prevail. This seemingly harmless idiosyncrasy actually sets the tone of Italian life as a society. As an inborn value it subliminally contributes to the lack of equality between men and women. Giovanna's assumption Mac should use the textbook, and I should happily and willingly take notes on a pad is an example. In her mind it was a perfectly natural solution.

This is how I as a female will be treated in future

situations. Should a question arise which needs an answer, it is most always directed to Mac, not me. If I happen to answer, the question might well be pointedly reasked to Mac. So subtly done, unless one is sensitive to such innuendos, the implication is totally missed. Obviously the Women's Liberation Movement has not made serious inroads on the Italian consciousness as yet.

ɕ

We both feel an urgency to start our language project. I think Giovanna has us a bit intimidated by stressing she is teaching a scholastic Italian, and her lessons will be thorough and difficult. Since she thinks it important to cover the entire textbook, we need to work fast. There is no time to waste. This is definitely pressure from teacher to student, and we sense it. Perhaps we should have waited until we each had textbooks. It is a week plus before the second one arrives.

ɕ

At our first class Giovanna teaches us the vowels, A,E,I,O and U. We quickly learn A sounds like ah, E sounds like pronouncing the letter a, I is like the letter e, O is oh, and U is ooh. It is easy, but one forgets the E and I sounds at first.

We then postpone Lezione Uno—io sono, tu sei—etc. in Parlo Italiano. We need to know food vocabulary so we can discuss with Dilia what we would like to eat. We learn the words for various meats, fruits, vegetables, plus bread, cheese and milk. We both take copious notes and have the words for a variety of foods to discuss with Dilia.

For good measure Giovanna teaches us the days of the week as well as the months of the year. That does not help with menu planning, but it is fun knowing them. Any small, but significant accomplishment makes you feel so good when you do not know even the simplest words.

One morning Dilia asks if she may have time off to visit her friend in Firenze. She claims driving there terrifies her, and so we are pleased she takes the initiative to go. This is her first time off since we arrived.

Early on the morning of her departure, before we are dressed, Dilia knocks at our bedroom door. Sante wants to move our car out of the way so he can get his ready for Dilia. Would we lend him the keys? Mac attempts to tell her to caution Sante about the thievery device on the ignition. Does she understand it has to be worked cautiously or it will freeze up and no one can start the car? Dilia nods she understands and will advise Sante.

Thievery devices on this Fiat Ritmo must be reckoned with each time the car is started. If your foot is on the foot-brake when the car is stopped, it will be impossible to restart the car. This is supposed to be a safety feature. Should, by mistake, your foot be on the foot-brake, and you wish to start the car, you pump the foot-brake and wait ten minutes. Then the car is suppose to restart as this frees up the system. If this is not complicated enough, there is an additional safety feature. One needs to use two keys in the ignition. If both are not quickly put in place when getting into the car, a shrill alarm goes off as a warning the car is being broken into! Everyone has trouble with this. One often hears the deafening sound of sirens in parking lots. Some driver, with door still ajar, is probably frantically leaning across the front seat trying to jab two keys into the ignition. It is comical when it is not your automobile.

ॐ

Mac and I hurry breakfast so Dilia and Massimo can leave. We plan to be at Giovanna's while they are away. Dilia locks every door in the Poggio. She bolts every window, upstairs and down, plus shuttering them. She stands by the dining room door, waiting for us to come out so she can lock it too. She is more than a little obsessed with security. The Poggio has never been as tightly latched during the daytime since we have lived there.

Massimo hops into their car, waiting for his mother. I await Mac by ours. He helps Dilia start her car, solemnly promising to close the gate when we leave. She drives out.

Mac gets into our car. Quickly he places both keys into the ignition and turns them on. The car does not start. He tries again. Still the car will not start. He gets out and raises the hood while asking me to help by turning the keys in the ignition. There is no spark. Mac is furious. He makes me promise never to let him lend the keys of this car to anyone again . . . He said he should have moved the car this morning instead of letting Sante do it. He had a hunch this would happen.

℅

What does one do when the car will not go, and the house is solidly locked, not even a window left unlatched? (We walked all around hoping to find some way to get back in.) One finds a telephone to call for help, but the nearest town is several miles away, and the neighbors are total strangers. The obvious solution is to introduce yourself to the neighbors and ask if you may use their telephone. This is the American way. Italians are apt to be suspicious of any newcomer. However, Mac walks down the road and knocks on the neighbor's door. He is greeted cautiously. He slowly explains in the most elementary Italian what has happened and asks if he may use the telephone. He adds Dilia is away from the Poggio, the place is locked, and we do not have a key.

When he mentions Dilia by name, the neighbor smiles and invites Mac into his home. Mac telephones the Hertz man who offers Mac advise: pump the brakes hard; wait ten minutes; then the car will start. Mac thanks him and makes a second call, this one to Giovanna so she will know what has happened and not worry when we do not arrive for our lesson. Giovanna does not drive so could not come to us.

72

Meantime I sit in the car and enjoy peace and quiet. I can hear birds singing and watch billowy white clouds move across blue sky. No Massimo shouting nor Radio Monte Carlo blasting. Not even Dilia's shoes clanking on stone floors. A most pleasant change.

Then Diavolo barks! Mac is walking on the road. Mac calls to the dog who wags his tail and is quiet. Mac gets into the car, explaining to me the procedure he is to follow. The prescribed ten minutes pass. He tries the ignition. The car will not budge. If possible the ignition works harder than before. The motor just does not ignite.

A very annoyed Mac realizes he must call the Hertz man once more. Since we have no idea when Dilia will return, we dare not wait for her to do our telephoning. By then the Hertz office may be closed for the day, and we would be without transportation tomorrow. Embarrassing as it is to ask the neighbors to use their telephone once again, it is the only possible solution.

This time the neighbor is delighted to see Mac. He had been picking cherries and offers some to eat. Mac thanks him and says he will bring some American potatoes to thank him properly for the cherries and the use of the telephone. The neighbor says that is such a big gift, he must give Mac some olive oil too. Mac enjoys this chatting, and apparently, so does the neighbor.

He returns to the Poggio to announce the Hertz people are bringing out another car. They will take this Ritmo back to Florence. We settle down and wait.

Suddenly, joyous barking from both dogs. Dilia and Massimo are back. No mistaking the meaning of those barks! Dilia drives in. She is astonished to see us. She is most upset we had such a difficult time with our car, but more especially we could not get into the house. We assure her we are fine and have everything under control.

❦

Later Mac tells me it took him thirty seconds to tell the Hertz man the way to get to the Poggio. No one has ever been able to give directions in thirty seconds before. Certainly never an Italian! The man is dumbfounded.

We learn the hard way if you ask an Italian directions, and he takes more than five minutes to tell you how to get there, he does not know what he is talking about. Do not follow his directions.

❦

The Hertz man appears and tries to start the car. He

fusses and fididdles, but he cannot make it ignite. Mac must drive with him back to Firenze in the automobile he brought so we can use that car tomorrow for own transportation.

A totally wasted day!

Eventually the Hertz people had to haul the Ritmo out by truck. The thievery device not only protected it from being robbed, it kept anyone from being able to drive the car at all.

🍂

Sometimes Massimo really can be a nuisance. He dashes into the room where Mac studies, grabs his clock/calculator, runs into the next room where I am studying, showing me the time. He tells me this in rapid Italian, which I do not understand. He dashes back to Mac and grabs our binoculars. He comes back, climbs up onto the long shelf that serves as my desk and opens the window directly in front of me. He puts the binoculars up to his eyes. He tells me all the things he is seeing in rapid Italian.

Having totally interrupted my work, I lean back in my chair to watch him and have to laugh. Our Massimo is looking through the large end of the binoculars, not realizing this is the wrong way to use them. What he sees must be very far away instead of very close up.

🍂

Each evening it is relaxing to have a drink in the living room before dinner. Dilia lights the fire, and we sit down by

75

it. Its warmth will be a luxury. Strange, almost immediately we feel cold, but neither of us want to admit it to the other. We pretend this is a warm, cozy interlude before dinner. Suddenly, we are so cold we cannot ignore the feeling and look at each other shivering.

The fire gives off no heat whatsoever! First, one of us, then the other takes turns leaning our behind into the fireplace as far as we dare. Soon we feel a little heat and quickly sit down, hoping this will help keep the warmth. Occasionally, we are almost comfortable.

⚬

Dilia's fires are built from olive tree prunings and old newspaper, scattered over the bottom of the fireplace in no set pattern. They seem to do more smoking than producing flames. We suspect the wood is green. The burning gives only the slightest heat. There is no real fireplace wood to use around that we can see.

⚬

On one particular evening we warmed ourselves especially well just before going into dinner. That evening we bundled up in our woolen sweaters and numerous other layers of the cotton clothing we had in our closets. As I lifted my fork to my mouth, I happened to hit the end of my nose. It was dripping and absolutely icy cold! I laughed.

"Imagine, Mac, here we are in sunny old Italy and simply

freezing. You know, none of our friends will believe this, will
they?"

Most people in the United States think springtime Italy is
warm and sunny. This is not true. Sadly it can be rainy too.
Warm weather comes in August and September.

One weekend we fly to Scotland. We need a change of
pace, and perhaps we have an inner yearning to hear the
sound of English. Our hotel, the Inverlochy Castle in Fort
William, has several wonderful fireplaces. Each evening they
are set with roaring fires. These simply mesmerize us. We
cannot stop staring at the spectacular flames and feel the
warmth flowing toward us.

When time comes to return to the Poggio, we ask the
concierge if we can buy some firewood to take with us. By
the look on his face we know he thinks this an odd request,
but he is too well trained to say so. He assembles a large box
of logs, all perfectly cut in the same length and of similar
diameter.

Dilia has never seen such wood for a fireplace fire. That
evening Mac insists on building it, and, for once, we have a
marvelous blaze which lights up the entire living room. Both
Massimo and Sante come to look at it. Dilia is so excited, she
gets out the iron grill for barbecuing. She rakes the coals
together and places her grill over them. There in our living
room she proceeds to cook steaks. Our Scottish fire made a
delicious dinner while we all savored its warmth.

Mac discovers the word distratto. A perfect example of its meaning is this story, which Giovanna tells us.

Giovanna says to her son, Didi, "Didi, please hand me the book."

Didi says, "yes," but he does not hand her the book.

Giovanna says to Didi a second time, "Didi, please hand me the book." Didi says, "yes," but still does not hand her the book.

A third time Giovanna says, this time loudly, "Didi, will you please hand me that book?" Didi, looking completely puzzled, says, "What did you say?"

That's distratto.

The classic example of distratto is told about Sir Isaac Newton cooking an egg. He puts his watch in the boiling water and looks at the egg in his hand to time when it will be done!

"Listen to Mr. Whiting, Mrs. Whiting," Giovanna says to me, unhappy with my pronunciation.

"Bellissimo, Mr. Whiting!" she says to Mac after his turn reading from the textbook.

"He has such talent, Mrs. Whiting."

℔

Giovanna has not much patience teaching a beginner. She is happiest when she can cover the lesson quickly and keep to her schedule.

I hint to Mac that I am falling behind. I am struggling to complete all the homework I missed by not having the textbook earlier. I am realizing what a disastrous beginning that made for me. He is thoroughly involved and enjoying himself. He has not noticed any problem and tells me not to be discouraged.

"Things will get better. You'll see," he assures me. "Soon all these lessons will begin to make sense."

I certainly hope this will prove true. Everything seems pretty complicated and disappointing right now. I am beginning to have ghastly nightmares in my sleep about being able to pronounce Italian beautifully only to awaken in a panic because my voice is not heard. I guess I can digest only so much. Maybe I should do some other things to break the tension I am feeling.

℔

One day we decide it is time to pick up la Signora's lamps on our way home from Giovanna's. Mac checks the map of Florence to see the route to take to find the store. It is indeed on our way back to the Poggio. No trouble at all for us to stop.

We leave Giovanna's a bit early in case something unforeseen should happen or the store should be closed if we are too late. We arrive in the vicinity to find all streets near the store one-way and going exactly the opposite direction from the one we are traveling. We must drive several blocks further along in order to get turned around into the proper area. Once accomplished there is no place to park! Around we go looking for a spot. Finally Mac drives down a narrow alley. There are a couple of cars parked along one side. He pulls in behind one and stops. This is probably illegal, (there is a sign ahead which we cannot read), but if I sit in the car, suggests Mac, perhaps everything will be fine. I smile and tell him to go on to the store.

§

I pick up my Italian textbook and start to work on tomorrow's lesson. Suddenly, a hand reaches into the open window on the driver's side and unlocks the hand brake of our car.

"Hey," I say in good old American slang, "what do you think you're doing?"

"Is ok, signora," says a total stranger, and he and his friend proceed to push our car down the street a few feet. Satisfied, they leave and walk back to a sliding door in the wall. One opens it while the other watches the street. A car is backed out, the door is relowered, and the two men drive away.

"Of all things!" I think to myself and resume studying.

Several other cars go down the street. It is a bit tricky passing me. There is hardly enough space for two cars. I expect Mac back soon and pay little attention. I am deeply engrossed in my Italian lesson.

Squeak, scrunch, squeak, some auto is abreast our car. I see the steel of my door bending in toward me! This automobile is big, too big to get by without damaging our car. Like a good Italian wife I lean out my window and bang the back fender of the car with my fist.

"What are you doing?" I yell in a loud voice at the driver. "Stop! You are denting my car!" I see it is an older model Mercedes with a young man driver at the wheel.

He stops the car and gets out.

"Oh, I am so sorry, Madame," he says in American accented English. "I didn't realize how tight this road is. This is my aunt's car. She lives up there a-ways in this neighborhood. I'm visiting her for the summer. She won't be too happy with this."

"I guess not. I'm not happy either. Now what are you going to do about this dent in my door?"

"Well, I guess I better try to go on since I am almost half way past you already. Is that ok, Madame? I am so sorry."

"Please give me your name and address first. This is a rented car, and we shall have to explain the dent to the Hertz people," I reply. "Do go very slowly. I don't want any more damage if possible."

He gets back in and literally creeps past me with no more abuse to our car, thank goodness.

༄

A few minutes later Mac reappears with the two lamps. "Here they are. Let's get going to the Poggio. Nothing unusual happened while I was away, did it?"

And I laugh as I start to explain.

༄

Finally one morning the sun is shining brightly and flows into the Pigeon Roost. Sitting at my typewriter, it warms my fingers on the keys and feels delicious.

I look out and see the tops of the olive trees gently swaying in the breeze, making a mass of silvery green. It is silent—not even a bird chirping.

Suddenly a coolish breeze blows in the window. A bird starts to sing. I smile to myself. How lucky to be here at this moment! I like this little room high above the rest of the Poggio. It is a place for seeing and feeling and being at peace with oneself and the world.

Contented I am!

༄

Clop, clop, clop! The sound of horses trotting down via di Riboia interrupts my musings. I look out the window and see a beautiful blonde woman riding past the Poggio, her groom slightly behind. Both are looking down the road and do not notice me watching them. We have never observed horseback riders here. I watch fascinated until they are out of sight.

I was told later the blonde is a contessa with a great personal tragedy in her life. Her only daughter, a teenager, recently was in a dreadful car accident. The girl is alive but will be crippled the rest of her life.

I cannot help wondering if she was wearing a seat belt . . .

*   *   *

Dilia is a natural born cook. Her food tastes simply delicious. When cooking, she never measures with a spoon or cup. She feels how it should be. She knows instinctively its taste. In my estimation no one can call himself a cook unless one can taste.

*   *   *

I watch Dilia make pasta. Using the kitchen table, she first covers it with a large, clean table cloth. Onto the middle of the cloth, she heaps flour, making a hole in its center with her fist. She breaks eggs and pours liquid into this hole. The flour and egg/liquid is mixed by pushing the flour from the outer edges of the cloth into the center with the egg/liquid. She keeps doing this by hand until it becomes a nice, fat ball of dough. She covers the ball with a cloth and allows it to rest on the table for a while. Next she kneads and pats and shapes the ball until its consistency feels right. She flattens it with a wooden roller until it is about an inch thick. She cuts the dough into strips. These are passed through a pasta roller, making thinner strips. She keeps rolling and rerolling until they are long and thin. They are left on the table while she steams fresh spinach on the stove. The spinach is barely cooked. She drains it thoroughly, then squeezes out the final bit of liquid with her hands. She puts it on her cutting board and chops it into small pieces with a huge knife. She divides the spinach into small portions, putting scoops evenly across the pasta. She covers them with another strip of dough. Taking a pizza cutting wheel, she draws squares around each portion. These are separated and allowed to dry slightly before they are plunged into boiling water to cook for our luncheon.

Dilia serves this pasta and a fresh tomato sauce topped with newly ground Parmesan cheese. What a treat, her spinaci ravioli! A treat watching Dilia create this. She never would allow me to help, but always made me feel welcome in her kitchen to observe. Great fun for me.

Electric pasta machines are new appliances not yet available in the United States. I am intrigued with them, but no self-respecting Italian housewife would have such a thing in her kitchen. One cannot feel the dough using such a machine. Her neighbors would say she is not a cook, a profound insult to any self-respecting Italian homemaker. Dilia does use an appliance called a passa tutto for pressing tomato pulp into puree and the roller to make her pasta into even size strips. These are acceptable appliances.

I eventually do buy a pasta maker. My neighbors will think it wonderful and want one for themselves.

☙

Alberto Fenyes suggests we each apply for a certificate called Permesso di Soggiorno. It is a document for foreigners who stay any length of time in Italy, giving legal proof that they are in residence. Such a document is recorded with the police. In his work at the Consulate Alberto has handled Americans who have gotten into trouble and need this authentication. He knows the difficulties that can arise out of not having one.

We are doubtful we shall be in Italy long enough to make this practical. We are not interested in involving ourselves in bureaucratic red tape. Alberto keeps urging us, however. He reasons should we have anything serious happen such as being robbed or being involved in an automobile accident, this document could help with identification and verification that we do have residency in the country. This is important. He thinks since we drive so much, it would be wise to have this security.

Each time we see him, he politely inquires if we have applied. He makes such a point of asking we finally decide to take his advice. Where should we go to apply for one? He suggests we check with the police in the city nearest the Poggio. That is Impruneta.

℃

To find the police station there takes a bit of searching. It is not on the main square, but down a side street and tucked around a corner. We go in the most likely entrance (it not being obvious that this is the entry) and are told by the young policeman in attendance to wait for the chief. After a few minutes a door is opened. We are invited into the room.

℃

Behind a huge wooden desk sits one small official. He is neatly dressed in formal uniform, his chief's hat poised at an angle on the desk in front of him. One knows while we are waiting in the anteroom, he is carefully grooming himself in that garb. He looks pressed and starched—an earnest man ready to give us his undivided attention. We have the impression he does not receive many formal callers, but he is very proud to do so.

Mac greets him and slowly in simple Italian tells why we came. He understands, but shakes his head. This is not the place to secure the permit. We must go into Firenze for such a document, to the central police station. "Where is that?" we ask. "In Firenze," he answers with a wave of his hand offering no specific directions on how to get there. Did we have recent photographs? We must have them. "Bon giorno, Signori!" We leave giggling. Such a lot of pomp and circumstance for what?

℃

For the price of one dollar it is possible to have four photos taken. One simply sits in a booth and pushes a button. What pictures! We decide if the Italian government wants anything better then they can do it for us. Armed with these and our passports we proceed to the central police station in downtown Florence.

Previously Alberto indicated which morning and at what time this office is open. We arrive in the vicinity of the station to find no parking space available and all streets one-way. Nothing to do except drive round and around until a spot opens up. The one we finally find is blocks from the station.

Walking into a huge building, we immediately see a long wooden table in an immense anteroom with three uniformed policemen sitting in chairs along the back. Mac approaches and asks in Italian where the Permesso Office might be. All three nod and say something which neither of us comprehend. We thank them and proceed to walk up the steps behind the table. We assume the office must be somewhere at the top. Half way up it dawns on us what they meant: The office is closed! The reason is totally obscure. Mac tries to ask the policemen at the table when it will be reopened. He is answered with shrugged shoulders. Possibly domani. Tomorrow?

Domani we try again. After the same drive to the station and the same parking problem, we finally are inside. The office is still closed. Today no one knows when it will reopen. Mac says something totally unprintable, and I certainly agree with him. We drive off to Giovanna's for our lesson in a huff! Our resolve to get this permit is weakening fast.

᪻

Kindly, persistent Alberto quietly convinces us and only because of him do we go once more. This time the office is open, and we get inside. What a tiny room for acquiring such an important document! There are two lines of people. I stand in one line with Mac in the other. Ahead of me are two Polish men. Their passports are labeled Polish/Czechvok. One man seems to be instructing the other. Ahead of Mac are four Italians. They are huddled over the barred window talking to the clerk on the other side. Two blacks are writing at one end of the only table in the room.

᪻

Mac reaches the head of his line first so I slip over beside him. The clerk says something we cannot understand. He says it three times. Still we do not fathom what he wants. He opens the grill and impatiently sticks his head out into the room. Very loudly he asks in Italian if anyone in the room can speak English? One of the blacks looks up and states he can.

This man explains to Mac and I in English that the official behind the grill wants to give us a blank form, which is to be filled out. He has been trying to give us that form. Once completed we are to attach our pictures and passport and return the forms to either man behind one of the two counters. Exactly one month from today our documents will be here to pick up. We thank him for the help and get out our pencils. Reading the form we find it mostly concerned with where we were born, of which country we are citizens, and more importantly, how we plan to support ourselves while living in Italy.

That's that. All the commotion and annoyance is to tell some official this information! We are none too pleased to be without passports for one month, especially the prospect of leaving them in this unorganized office. We hand the clerk our filled-in forms and leave with the apprehension we shall never see any of it again.

We have lived here one month, a busy month, and it is still cold! We are becoming impatient with this intemperate springtime. No warm, balmy days of sunshine—certainly no dining on our loggias or going on a picnic. We wonder whether the weather shall ever warm up. We are annoyed with cold, rainy days which seem to continue on and on. Mac studies the construction of the Poggio, trying to determine why we are so uncomfortable inside too. Although its walls are thick, they do not seem to be properly insulated. They leak air. Sometimes the air becomes a breeze. We know they could have benefited from a good layer or two of styrofoam insulation. It is way too late for that.

Slowly, slowly he steers through. Benissimo, Frederico!

"What can possibly be at the end of this miserable road?"

Opening the gate to the Poggio.

A profusion of wisteria blooms in the springtime.

Furniture store in Florence stocked full of good-looking wicker pieces.

Loggia with ping-pong table.

We begin by establishing a seating arrangement around the fireplace.

We are developing a friendly student-teacher relationship.

All of a sudden the aroma of Wrigley's Juicy Fruit chewing gum seems to be surrounding me!

Giovanna, her huge smile makes her olive brown eyes crinkly and friendly.

From the fascination of collecting wood for our front door led to this collection of photos I took of old Italian ones.

Iris is light lavender.

Italy's most common wildflower, the ginestra.

Dilia patiently interprets our attempts to speak her language. So does every Italian we encounter. People smile when we try conversing and often help with a word or phrase. This happens after only a few lessons. It is a great feeling. Important for us to keep in mind the reason we are taking lessons is to communicate. Maybe we are becoming so bogged down with the academic and perfect pronunciation we may be overlooking this simple truth. One observes little children who have never been to school quite easily chit-chatting with anyone they choose. We need to adopt more of this same ease. So, relax, Helen! Relax, Mac! Little by little it will come.

꜡

We know a lot more words than we do grammar, what we think we say is not always what we do say. Dilia keeps the trusty Italian/English dizionario nearby. That and her big smile encourage our efforts.

꜡

One morning I happily bounce down the staircase with its eighteen stone steps, turn at the bottom and walk into the kitchen for breakfast.

"Buenos dias, Dilia," I greet her.

Dilia is much too polite to tell me I am saying good morning in some language other than Italian!

꜡

Mac loves the learning challenge. Outside the classroom he deliberately gets himself involved in the most complicated conversations to test his new skill. We both thoroughly enjoy this repartee. It proves the lessons are worthwhile. While Mac is contented learning to speak, I am intrigued by the music of the words. Sometimes, not knowing the proper way to answer Massimo, I sing a reply, using sounds to express myself. Amazingly, he understands. Massimo speaks no English, and still we are communicating. Sometimes when I want to tell him a special thing, I speak very seriously in

English and look directly at him. I pretend he understands exactly what I am saying. He answers back in Italian very seriously, looking directly at me. He pretends I know exactly what he is saying. Then we laugh. It is a game we both enjoy.

᪥

A definition: a villa is a country home with a garden and a view. We see so many, we look up the meaning in the dizionario. From a distance villas can always be spotted as the large ones which have the long driveways. Both sides of the drive are solid with plantings of cypress trees. These slender cipressi are old, tall and terribly dignified, I think.

᪥

Each morning as we start eating breakfast, a loud voice shouts from Dilia's apartment. It is Massimo. He wants us to know he is awake.

His mother shouts back to him, "Vengo, Massimo! I'm coming."

This exchange goes on several more times. Along with the loud Monte Carlo jazz from the radio, we are wide awake too.

Allora! Well, then.

᪥

One morning we are eating and more or less listening to Monte Carlo when the announcer says, " . . . dedicated to Dilia Casini . . . Impruneta." We could not catch all the Italian in between. We did understand a song is dedicated to Dilia. She blushes and turns toward the sink as it is played, keeping her back to us. She is embarrassed but will never forget the recognition.

☙

One day Mac looks up from his textbook and says to me, "Buon giorno, la cara mia signora di colore di giallo banana."

"What did you say?" I ask, startled.

"Good morning, my dear sweet, banana yellow-colored wife!"

"Mac!" I laughingly exclaim. "This Italian has gotten to you!"

☙

Massimo has a two-wheel bicycle. It has tiny wheels and hand brakes. The seat has been raised for Massimo's long legs. He drives this bike like a professional car racer, a small demon on wheels, zooming around at a furious rate. He adores pedaling directly at something or someone. At the last possible moment he slams on the brakes, screeching to a sliding stop. This is especially satisfying when he is on the gravel of the driveway, as he can spray a lovely shower of small pebbles all over the lawn.

I have watched him barely miss a head-on crash into a tree, saw him narrowly avoid cracking the huge sliding glass door of the living room, miss hitting Mac, and both cats. So far he has never hit anything or anybody, but not for lack of trying.

Massimo, so fierce looking on his tiny two-wheeler, one forgets he is very skilled handling this vehicle at his age.

☙

Mac calls Massimo, "Piccolo Fagiolo." Massimo grins and calls Mac, "Grande Fagiolo." They both laugh and think this is so funny, the Little Bean and the Big Bean. They are becoming good friends.

☙

Mac decides to photograph the Poggio thoroughly. Massimo wants to help. Everywhere Mac goes, Massimo tags along. Mac is polite but does not encourage his companionship.

One particular picture Mac wants is of the roof outside the upstairs guest bedroom. The way the tiles have been laid to slant downward is especially beautiful. Massimo pulls a chair up to the window Mac opened and starts to climb out onto the roof.

Mac tells him no firmly, but gently. Massimo pays no attention.

Back up the chair, out the window and onto the roof

Massimo moves, quick as lightning. Mac grabs him, lifts him out of the window and back down to the floor.

"No, Massimo!" he tells him, louder and firmer than before.

Again Massimo pays no attention, and a third time proceeds to climb out the window.

This time Mac grabs him roughly and says in a loud, strong voice, "No, Massimo, you cannot do that!"

Massimo's face crumbles. His eyes turn coal-black. He stamps his foot. He is furious with Mac and stands nearby, glowering at him. Mac pays no attention to his tantrum. Massimo does not try to climb out the window again.

Calmly Mac finishes photographing. He closes the window and pulls its shutter. He does not want to be responsible if a determined little boy decides he will climb out that window when the signori are not around.

We can always tell when it is a bad day outside. The two dogs stay in their houses. Diavolo and Tome have strange lives. Both are tied with a long rope, the end fastened to a stake pounded in the ground at the front of each house. Each rope is long enough for the dog to walk entirely around his house.

Walk around their house. That is all they have to do all day long. They are never untied. Diavolo, the younger dog, has some spirit. He becomes excited when strangers walk by the Poggio and barks loudly. Both are fed sparingly, in our estimation starvation rations.

Tome is old and quiet and listless. Sante told us he was a great hunting dog when he was younger. We worry because he is extremely thin, actually skin and bones. He is unpleasant to look at. Sante says all hunting dogs are kept thin as they work better.

We wonder. Would seem kinder to put him to sleep than have him go on living like this.

🙰

Several nights I awake to the sounds of cats fighting outside our window. I mention this to Dilia. She says it is not cats fighting but il gulfo, the owl hooting. This owl lives somewhere in our roof. We never find him although we try.

🙰

Dilia calls her female cat cicciona, by which she means, fat lady, shortening it to Cina. In the same vein the male cat should be ciccione, but Dilia never calls him fat man. He is just il gatto, and we suspect she merely tolerates him. We call them il gatto or la gatta and constantly mix up which is which.

🙰

Cina hid her off-springs in a place no one discovered. She is a smart gatta who knows her babies will be destroyed if

97

found. Il gatto, on the other hand, is altogether dumb. In Italian one would say, stupido! He is the cat who caught his leg in the trap in the field. He is the cat who allows Massimo to catch him. Cina never lets Massimo near her. She is the cat Massimo chased with the pruning shears when we first inspected the Poggio some months past. She always leads the way when the two cats walk around together.

⌘

It is a dilemma whether to open the bedroom window or not before going to sleep. Cats may take advantage and come in. Occupants have been wakened up to find cats in the room and unhappily witnessed the welter weight exchanges peculiar to the cat world.

⌘

Se fosse fatto, sarebbe bene, sarebbe fatto rapidamente. "If t'were done, t'were well, t'were done quickly!" A little Italian Shakespeare, courtesy of Mac.

⌘

Still the easiest way to check vocabulary is speaking to Massimo. If what we say is correct, he pays attention. Should we say something using the wrong word, he totally ignores us. He is beginning to answer me. I am pleased as this means

98

I sound more Italian. A proud, hard-won accomplishment.

ᕯ

One day Massimo invades the Pigeon's Roost. He knows he is not to bother me when I am there. Of course, no four year old's mind contains the word never. I hear him coming, but pretend I do not and continue working on the typewriter. Suddenly he is beside me, his chubby, little finger poised above the on/off key of the machine. I continue typing, ignoring him. He pushes the button. The machine stops.

I look at Massimo and say sternly, "No. Don't do that. Please turn it back on."

Massimo looks at me smiling with all the charm and charisma of a grownup Italian dandy.

"Signora," he says, blinking black eyes at me, "vuole una tazza di caffe?" Do *you* wish a cup of coffee?

I blink back at him, and say very seriously, "Massimo, vuole una tazza di caffe?" Do *you* wish a cup of coffee?

He laughs delighted. Pointing his finger at me, he says, "Non, lei!" No, *you!*

ᕯ

There is a rat-a-tat-tatting somewhere in the upstairs sitting room. At first we think our ears are hearing odd noises. When the sound becomes constant, our curiosity gets the better of us, and we decide to locate it. In the wooden ledger above the door to the dressing room is our noisemaker.

We listen. "Tat-a-tat." It is unfailing in its consistency.

A termite, we decide. Friendly soul! He works all hours, but seems most active during daylight. We are grateful for that.

☙

A scuolabus is a minibus used for taking children to school. Next year one will stop at Massimo's door and pick him up too. These buses, although somewhat small in size, are painted bright, shiny yellow. Sometimes we wish Massimo could be going to school this year. So full of energy, he can be tiring to have around all day. He seems ready, but Italian children do not start school until they are five years old. There are no day care centers for working women's children. Should a mother not be able to care for her own, Grandma or another relative is pressed into service—never a stranger.

☙

Massimo has a fine time playing cars and trucks. He lines them up on the terrace wall. There must be dozens. They look impressive sitting there. He plays all sorts of games with them. When he is bored, he simulates a huge wreck. Cars and trucks scatter all over the terrace. A marvelous catastrophe to behold!

☙

"Pronto, signori!" "Ready, sirs!" Each evening this is the way Dilia calls us to dinner. She is serious. She likes to serve her food hot, right from the stove. Occasionally, just as Dilia is ready to serve dinner, Mac receives an overseas telephone call. Usually this is from Bob Anderson who is constructing our new home in Idaho. The problem lasts long enough for Dilia to begin wringing her hands: her dinner is getting cold. After these calls happen several times in a row, Dilia shakes her head, looks at me and says, "Signor Anderson. Si, I know." "Yes, I know."

Suddenly they come. One night we are asleep, and the next morning both of us have red, itchy bumps on arms and faces. We show these to Dilia, and she moves into action. Out come little square boxes with electrical cords called vape. She strategically places one in each bedroom, plugging it into a wall outlet. Its center has a tiny hollow place where she inserts a small pellet. A vapor is produced, which we cannot detect. The gnat population is now under control, she announces.

Thinking this helps control the insect population is a little like believing in the tooth fairy. We'll see.

We have an opportunity to ship our three paintings back home. They will be taken from Florence to Geneva and transported to the United States from there. Such a simple way! We have them driven to the airport in Florence for customs clearance. Customs asks where they have originated. No painting can go out of Italy without origin papers as they might be stolen Italian art of great value. Back they come. Our origin papers are in the United States.

☙

Mac calls Alberto at the Consulate to say what happened and ask what he can do to help. Alberto carefully explains the procedure. First they should go to a carpenter to have wooden crates made. The crates must be constructed in such a way so they can be opened for inspection. Mac thinks Sante can build these at the Poggio, but Sante does not have any wood. Mac needs to find a professional carpenter who does have wood to do the job. Sante suggests where to go.

☙

When Mac meets the carpenter, they agree two boxes are necessary and on which day the boxes might be completed. This last is bargainable. Afterwards, Alberto said, the paintings in their new crates are to go to Belli Arte. Customs require the Belli Arte people to look at each painting. They decide its significant value to the Italian culture which determines whether it can or cannot leave the country.

☙

Mac is much annoyed at the large size and the elaborateness of the crates. He has to hire a van to carry them to Belli Arte. The crates are too large to fit into our Fiat. Upon inspection Belli Arte says our paintings are not Italian cultural artifacts and therefore are of no interest to them. They do insist Mac must show them to Dogana Centrale. Dogana Centrale is in another section of Florence on the other side of the city. When we find the place, those officials tell Mac if Belli Arte has no interest in our paintings, they certainly are not interested either. Signor Whiting is free to export them without further discussion.

All this red tape for nothing! Mac is exhausted and disgusted from running around. So much for origin papers too!

The two crates cost one hundred dollars apiece plus an untotaled amount of lira for renting the van. We learn the hard way what not to bring to Italy another time.

Suddenly living here becomes totally exasperating! Dilia, Massimo, the driving, our lessons, the weather—each seem to be making little problems that are creeping into the joy of our daily life. They are irritating us beyond all proportions to their worth. The need to talk about these frustrations is overwhelming. One longs for a compatible friend from home to help laugh them away. The plain fun of living in a foreign country has dulled. Both Mac and I are uptight and bad-tempered. We must get rid of these sour feelings so we can enjoy the rest of our stay.

We have learned visiting and residing in Italy are two entirely different situations. When visiting, either as a guest at someone's home or at a hotel, one is not involved in the nitty-gritty of daily life. Taking the responsibilities for a residence, either renting as we are doing, or owning outright, the day-to-day problems cannot be ignored, much as one might wish them away. There is always some little matter begging for attention. It is that attempt to solve the difficulty with reasoning understood by the Italian mentality which tests nerves and patience. We cope by being flexible and resilient. This simplest of solutions is the hardest to achieve, but we are learning. We are trying to laugh the tenseness away too. Laughter is the greatest antidote there is. It is ridiculous to allow our time here to become so serious, but we cannot pretend to be casual tourists any longer. Our life has too much structure to use this as an excuse.

℥

While pondering these emotions to excise them, I suddenly remember a group of women I knew several years ago. All of them had made homes in foreign lands for their families much like we are trying to do at the Poggio. Their husbands worked for the same company as Mac did. Many were raising very young children. In that particular era they may not have had too much choice whether to uproot their families to the foreign place. In those times when the husband's expertise was needed, the whole family transferred to the locality where he did the job. I think now of their willing spirits and am full of admiration. How difficult the

106

adaptation must have been for them. Undoubtedly many of their experiences were similar to some of ours here at the Poggio. This is an ideal opportunity to sit in the Pigeon's Roost and think about them.

ℰ

Mac's work took him to all the continents—sometimes more than once a year. He was needed in Europe—Zurich, London, Paris, Milan, Livorno, Athens, Bilbao, Stade, Stockholm, Copenhagen, and Terneuzen. He traveled to the Mid-East—Istanbul, Tehran, Tel Aviv, and Amman, Jordan. In Africa he went to Algiers, Johannesburg, and Lagos. Tokyo, Hong Kong, Taipei, Kuala Lumpur, Jakarta, Manila, Bangkok, Bombay were the Asian stops, as well as Sydney and Melbourne in Australia and Plymouth and Wellington in New Zealand. South America it was Bogota, Rio de Janeiro, Buenos Aires, Sao Paolo, Quito, Lima, and Santiago, and finally Mexico City in Central America. It was a time-consuming, strenuous, but fascinating type of job.

ℰ

I went along with Mac to have a life with my husband, but quite on my own initiative began knowing many company wives. Some were transferees from the United States. Others were nationals from whichever country we happened to be visiting. Quite suddenly the most rewarding hours of the trip for me became those I spent with them.

There was always so much laughter in our associations. This might be in their home or my hotel room or driving here and there to whatever was planned for that day.

⚜

A few specific events come into my mind . . .

A treasured happening in Tokyo: My hostess and I were invited to the studio of a master craftsman who, while we sat in total silence and watched in awe, delicately transplanted a very large, ancient, and extremely rare bonsai tree into a new pot—using only chopsticks!

⚜

Another time a large group of we women went to the famous Japanese Kabuki theater. I had never been and watched wide-eyed. I thought it absolutely marvelous! (Its formality seemed almost Shakespearean to me.) Then something about its style hit my funny-bone. I had trouble controlling the giggles which bubbled up from the depth of my stomach causing some of the other women to giggle too. It is a wonder we were not asked to leave. We were very rude.

⚜

Such ambiance that production had! Its cast was all male actors, and their impersonation of the female outstanding, a major reason for attending Kabuki. One first notices the marvelous makeup on the actors is from the era of the ancient imperial court. It is theatrical and stylized. Then one hears the voices, playing the women in the play. They project across the stage in squeaky, high pitched tones to imitate a female. The costuming is the old court style, and the kimonos in sumptuous satins and brocades have beautiful flowing trains. The actors wearing these have on stilted shoes, making their walking possible only with tiny, little mincing steps. Each sentence of the dialogue is repeated three times and uttered with a particular roll of the actor's head, his interpretation of how a court lady acts. Then the clang of a cymbal is heard. This is to announce a set change. Invisible scene changers appear in the background. They are dressed totally in black leotards, head to toe, and crawl around the stage moving the scenery. "But, I see them quite plainly," I said to our guide. "Oh, no you don't," she replied. "They are invisible because they are dressed in black. You understand?"

A later time this same tiny little intelligent guide, who gave us so many hours of pleasure learning about her Japan, announced she was going to be married. "That's wonderful!" we exclaimed. "Do tell us about the man you are marrying." "Oh, I don't know him," she replies. "My family is arranging it." "How do you know you will be happy with a man you have never met?" we brazenly ask. "Oh, my family will decide that. They know me best and will choose someone who is right for me," she answers with absolute confidence. She is a good Japanese daughter.

Sometimes on other trips I became involved in courses or events of current interest to my hostess, like a dog obedience class in Mexico City. Those animals understood their commands which was infinitely more Spanish than I knew.

Many times it was my pleasure to play and chat with my hostess's children. Once in Buenos Aires I chaperoned a family of eight who only spoke Spanish (which I do not) to the afternoon cinema. We had a great time, ate a lot of candy, and I did get them all safely back to their mother!

My mind returns to the present. From the very first we recognize the key to successful living in our particular Italian countryside would involve solving the language problem. When we learn we are a part of a neighborhood with not one person who could speak a word of English, it is a shock. We realize not knowing any Italian will develop into a crisis of major proportion. Confronting this barrier on a daily basis is a lonely and sobering experience. How frustrating it is to be in a house and not be able to communicate with the housekeeper even about the simplest of things. Learning Italian quickly is our number one priority. This is an uphill fight every waking hour.

℥

I once asked a wife who had recently moved to a rather remote area how everything was coming along for her. She indicated quite well. Then she said, "But I have a maid!"

"Well, is that so terrible?" I asked.

"Oh, no," she answered, "it should be wonderful, but I cannot communicate with her!"

Deja vu! Our daily frustration at the Poggio. We have a wonderful maid, Dilia, and we cannot talk with her either!

℥

Our Dilia is both a joy as well as an irritation. Talented a housekeeper as she is, she tends to bustle about, her wooden shoes clanking noisily on the Poggio's stone floors. We always can hear where she is. She is a very much in-charge person who wants to do every task herself. She is well trained, and she expects to go about her business without any interference from us. I, for instance, like to press my clothing. (How this amuses my daughters who regard this job as unnecessary nonsense rather than one of the household arts!) I suggested to Dilia I would like to do this, but she was horrified. Indignant as a plump little bantam hen, she gave

111

me to understand she had time to do my ironing. She totally misunderstood I wanted (and needed) a household task for my own satisfaction. It certainly was not her image of "la signora." Secretly I had also hoped to speed up the laundry process. One waits three or four days to get a clean garment back into one's closet. Italian housekeepers do not like electric driers so Mother Nature does the drying. With our rainy weather this takes time. Another household task I adore is arranging bouquets of flowers. After her reaction to my desire to iron, I did not dare suggest this to Dilia! No matter how much I missed having something special to do in the household, I would not have intentionally insulted Dilia for anything in the world.

Mac feels the same constraint. He needs to do something domestic. He hardly contains himself at the way Dilia builds the fires in the fireplace. When he tries to help, she brushes him aside. She takes it as a personal criticism if we want to do anything she regards as her work. Since Sante cares for the outside, there is nothing Mac can contribute to this either.

We chaff at a lack of participation in our own home, but recognize the Poggio is Dilia's and Sante's responsibility. Neither of us are comfortable with much pampering.

℅

Both Mac and I like children and miss our own whenever we travel. Initially we were so pleased to find a little boy at the Poggio. Now little Massimo has become a pleasant nuisance! We enjoy him, and he likes us, but he has difficulty leaving us alone. We have a lot of trouble doing anything without having him tag along. He is a hyperactive child who can never do things quietly. When he is awake, we all know. How enjoyable less noise would be as well as no little trailing shadow!

℗

The Poggio's owner once questioned me if I thought Massimo was normal. I replied I certainly did and asked her what did she mean "normal?" She suggested his hyperactivity might be a sign of mental instability. I assured her we found him most intelligent. Indeed, once we brought him an erector set of building materials. How quickly he went about constructing an airplane! We do think he should be in school or at least in more contact with other children his own age. At the Poggio are only adults. We have seen no children in this neighborhood.

℗

"Why are we expending so much effort to learn a language?" I quiz myself, thinking of our daily Italian lessons. Learning this Italian has now become such a ponderously deadly task, rather than an interesting project. Never had I let language deter me from speaking when I traveled with Mac.

℗

We went to a company party one evening in Buenos Aires. Several of the men knew English, but none of the women. They only spoke Spanish. I was seated with them for the evening and enjoyed talking with them the full six hours we were at the party. They did not understand my English nor I their Spanish yet we had marvelous conversation and a laughing, wonderful time.

☙

I had a complicated, but interesting language time in Algeria too. Mac was off to the desert with the men, and I stayed in Algiers. (The bathtub in my hotel room was so long and so deep I literally was afraid I might slip and drown when it is filled. And, Winston Churchill had secretly stayed at this same hotel at the height of the Second World War. A plaque marks his room. It is across the hall from mine.) My plans were to sightsee with two of the company women. One was French from Paris who spoke some English, but no Algerian. The other was Algerian who spoke some French, but no English, and I who spoke only English. What an interesting two days of sightseeing fascinating Roman ruins built on black sandy beaches we three had without a moment's hesitation in the conversation!

☙

The language barrier occurred again in Taipei, Taiwan. Mac and I and the three other men with whom we are traveling were invited to dinner at the home of the company's agent. We arrived and were invited to be seated at a chest high, round Chinese table with a sizable lazy Susan in its center. Several other Chinese are guests, but our hostess and I were the only women present. In front of each of us was a small silver round plate, a tiny silver goblet, and a set of ivory chopsticks. We were entertained for the next several hours by the most elaborate feast any of us had ever seen. There was a succession of more than twenty different courses from every type of Chinese cuisine. Some dishes were cooked at the table by our hostess using various types of fascinating cooking equipment and utensils. It was a feast for the eye as well as the palate. There was no common language, but much conversation with nods and bows. We were toasted by our host and hostess and returned the same using the little silver goblets. Whiskey was the beverage served, and I came home having had a fabulous time, but with a huge thirst!

Which reminds me of a funny dinner party in Hong Kong. It was held at the apartment of a Chinese business-man, who was a good plastics customer. To reach the apartment we were escorted into the freight elevator of a tall building. His plastics plant was the bottom part of the building, and his residence was the penthouse on top. We are warmly greeted at the front entrance by our host and his Chinese wife. She is in a pale jade green traditional high-necked silk chi-pao dress with skirt slit to her thigh. While she nods to us, she has little to say. I notice the front of her

115

dress is stained with spots. Shanghai crab was the piece de resistance that evening. Much fanfare brings forth the platters of crabs. There is a heated discussion between the men about the sex of each crab, which distresses the women. We preferred eating them without such knowledge . . . Three nights later at a restaurant in Hong Kong we entertain this same gentleman and his wife. In they walk, and we rise to greet them. The wife is traditionally dressed in a navy crepe chi-pao. A large spray of sapphires and diamonds is pinned to her spotless bosom. This wife is not the same person we met at the apartment a few nights previously. This is the city wife and is concubine number two!

❦

The language lesson learned in our travels has never let not understanding words be a barrier to enjoying interesting opportunities when they arise.

❦

Now our intense concentration to learn proper Italian with Giovanna makes it necessary to devote most of the day to studying. Those academic seven or eight hours, five days a week is a lot of time to spend on one subject even for the most ardent student. The brain gets tired! Our weekends away are welcome diversions although most of them are to places similar to living at the Poggio. More variety in our daily life would be a good idea, but there are precious few hours left from studying to do anything of significance. Working at a less hectic pace might make learning easier and be a lot more fun for me at least.

℥

That drive to and from Giovanna's apartment, a short half hour, was one of the most unnerving jaunts imaginable. It certainly did not help arriving at Giovanna's in a relaxed mood for our lesson. The quickest route straight through Florence was always full of hectic traffic. Nighttimes as we returned to the Poggio, we felt very fatigued after our language session. In this mood we met the full blast of every other Italian rushing home too. It was wild motoring and took concentrated effort of both the driver and his passenger to endure with any peace of mind.

℥

Day in, day out our most persistent irritation is the miserable chilly, rainy weather. It is demoralizing our spirits. We are plain cold much of the time in spite of warm sweaters and the stufa. We should confront Dilia so she understands how uncomfortable we really are. How much more pleasant the Poggio would be by starting the furnace, legal or not. Our morale would be considerably lifted by the comfort of a warm home. We did not wish to provoke any unpleasantness with Dilia about this. No doubt we were acting American foolish by not complaining aloud to her.

117

Forever the optimists we keep rationalizing the weather will change. Our stufa in the small sitting room maintains some warmness, but basically we awake cold, study cold, and eat cold. We bed early because it is too cold anywhere in the house to sit up and read or chat. The consequence of this is we never are totally relaxed in this atmosphere.

＊

My mind drifts to other memories. Thinking about them is like a breath of fresh air for me. They put our present problems at the Poggio into balance.

＊

I started a collection of wood in Australia. Ultimately this became an important part of our home in the United States. Before beginning any traveling with Mac, I asked the architect of our home in a casual way what I might bring back from all the places we would be going that might be used in our home. He thought for a moment, then surprised me enormously by replying, "wood."

"But, Alden, what are we going to do with wood?" I asked intrigued. Our home is completely built.

In his quiet thoughtful way he said, "We'll design a front door!"

＊

And so it started. Every country I went to I asked my hostess where I could acquire a piece of wood native to that country. My first try was in Australia. Undaunted by the request my friend said she thought we should go to a timber mill. She then lectured to me about the trees native to Australia so I would have some idea what to ask for once we got there.

"Where is this lumber mill?" I asked when she finished her recital.

"Oh, Helen, in Australia it is called a 'timber mill'. A 'lumber mill' does not refer to milling wood, and we shall find it just down this road."

At the "timber mill" we walk up a steep staircase which is open on one side to the outdoors into a simple office at the top. There sits a secretary at a desk, and a man standing talking on the telephone. The girl looks up, and we tell her what we want. The man hangs up the telephone and faces us.

"So, you want a piece of gum wood? Whatever for?" he asks. Clearly he is flabbergasted at having two completely unknown young women walk unannounced into his office and ask for a piece of Australian gum. He is the owner of the mill.

I explain. He is so intrigued he picks up a crosscut saw and takes us himself through his large mill. Every so often he stops, picks up a board and saws a piece off, identifies it, then hands it to me. We collect an armful. When we leave, he is laughing and shaking his head.

That was the beginning of what turned into a huge collection of interesting woods from every part of the globe. The sum total resulted in a handsome front door for the Whiting home. This door is an artistic combination of pieces of all the woods I collected. It is unusual and quite beautiful.

That same Australian lady knew the zoo keeper in Sydney too. Would I be interested in going to the zoo she asked me one day. They had a very good collection of Australian animals there. I most certainly would! To my absolute surprise and delight she had prearranged with the zoo keeper, who was a friend of hers, for me to hold a koala bear! I can still feel that soft cuddly animal who put his arms around my neck and snuggled against me. He went sound to sleep with his long front tooth pressed against my throat. How delicious he smelled of the eucalyptus leaves he had been eating.

I went back to Sydney and bought toy koala bears for our children.

My friend loved her proper English tea. She and her husband traveled with us to Melbourne. She came down to the lobby the next morning simply incensed. "Whatever is wrong?" I asked her."

"This hotel! I'll never stay here again," she sputtered.

"They served me early morning tea with a tea bag!"

‍🍃

My English friends and their tea. Another in London was absolutely horrified when served cream with hers. Cream in tea?

Oh my goodness!

‍🍃

We thought we were being robbed in tiny New Plymouth, New Zealand. Waking up early one morning we heard footsteps coming into our room. I pulled the sheet over my head, but peaked out from a crack. A person came right up between the two beds and deposited something on the table beside them. "What in the world is that?" we both say, bolting upright in our beds after the person left. It was morning tea, served on a nice tray with cups and sugar and hot milk. Bringing it to our room first thing in the morning was a local custom!

‍🍃

The New Zealanders made much ado of a passion fruit puree for a special treat at what they called tea, but was actually what we know as supper. Politely eating that seedy stuff did not add to our enthusiasm for being there.

Somehow they had the idea I was a trained horticulturist so all sorts of plants and flowers and vegetation were being brought to me for inspection. We appreciated their thoughts however mistaken they were in their assumptions.

᪥

Often terribly funny things happen when traveling. We were in Bangkok being driven to a pharmaceutical plant. Two company women greet our arrival. One tours us through the plant. We observe the process of making pills.

"Please, have one," she offers proudly as we view the end product.

"But, what are they for?" we ask hesitant to eat an unknown medicine.

"Oh, worms!" she says, adding, "they work very well too!"

᪥

I salute all these women and many others I knew. How I admire their spirit and enjoyed their friendship! These reminiscences have brightened my spirits immeasurably. They make our Italian complaints now seem very small indeed. How important it is to take time to think! It is difficult to comprehend present situations as stressful when living here seems so easy. I laugh aloud and feel refreshed and alive. I know we can overcome any Italian frustration with the sureness that comes from experience.

❦

In spite of the language barrier, Dilia, Massimo, the driving, and the constantly miserable weather, we never waver from our original decision to fulfill the three months lease agreement. I am flabbergasted to realize any single one of those problems had the potential to drive us back to the comfort of our home in the United States. This possibility never crosses either of our minds. That is a source of pride to both of us.

❦

Two whole months have totally passed since we took residency at the Poggio. We know how it feels to be deflated, but not defeated! This is what happens when one seeks challenge. We got more than we had anticipated. That by far is the greatest gift of all.

❦

We will spend two weeks at the Excelsior Hotel in Florence before returning to the United States. We look forward to this. Staying in the urban atmosphere of Firenze will bring our Poggio adventures into proper perspective. That outlook will help us recognize what a rewarding experience these past months have been.

In Italy driving a car is not a means of getting from here to there. It is a competitive sport scary for the faint-hearted like me but much fun for one who loves to drive like Mac.

᪄

This is what it feels like to be his passenger. He starts the car, stops the car, shifts the clutch, brakes quickly, then reshifts. Bumpy going this shifting! Jerky too. The car seems to sway a lot. Aperto/chiuso? The sign flashes by too quickly to tell which fuel station is, open or closed. A gloved Mac drives, the road map held in his left hand along with the steering wheel. He shifts gears with his right hand which also manages the turning signal and windshield washer. He uses the washer often because he cannot stand a dirty windshield. Says it ruins his vision, but he hates hearing the wiper run all the time so he flips it on and off when the glass gets a few spots. On a rainy day he does this flipping too. On/off, on/off it goes adding to the general commotion. Whenever some difficult maneuver lies ahead, Mac hits the right side of his nose with his fist, then goes into action. A signal to me that he is concentrating hard.

ह

Giovanna says, "You know, Mr. Whiting, after ten minutes of looking, I left the address at home. I could not find it. I am absolutely certain I know where the place is. Well, ninety five percent certain."

We are looking for her water supplier to buy bottled water because Giovanna says hers is cheaper than ours so we should buy from him.

"But, Giovanna," sputters Mac, "a road has a beginning and an ending. The trick is to know which is which." We are driving round and around the neighborhood, not finding the supplier. "How do you recognize which is which?"

"Well, Mr. Whiting, that's not hard for us. We Italians just know!" answers Giovanna.

"Do we go east or west on this street, Giovanna?" Mac is getting frustrated.

"Mr. Whiting, in Italy we are not that precise!"

After many twists and turns we do discover where we are supposed to be. The place is almost where Giovanna said although not quite.

༉

Traffic does not flow in straight, organized lines with one car following another. It is a conglomeration of every sort of vehicle from bicycle to heavy-duty truck all determined to reach their destination first. This means outdriving everyone. Vehicles jam tightly together on city streets, unevenly side by side and bumper to bumper.

We whiz along winding in, out, and around. Occasionally Mac takes his eyes off the road to point at something he sees which he thinks I will find interesting. Looking away from the cars ahead makes me nervous. I watch how we progress as if I am at the wheel. In this mass of traffic I am scared to look elsewhere.

It is quite normal to have the driver in the car on your right side, suddenly turn left directly in front of you. The reasoning behind this is the car on his left is probably turning left too! That sort of logic makes Italian driving a challenge.

༉

At a stop light it is a cultural aberration if the last man to reach the light is not the first man through the intersection. If the last man has not taken to the sidewalk in order to preserve his prerogative, he has proved himself unworthy of his heritage!

☙

One never knows in the suburbs what may come around a blind curve, and there are many of these. Italian drivers blow the horn, keep their foot on the accelerator and zoom on. Often they are not on their own side of the road. The assumption is the other fellow will move over.

☙

Some smaller European cars seem unsteady on the highway. They sway as they are driven. Italian country roads are never level. Your body wrenches from side to side. It is particularly noticeable on roads with many curves and bends.

☙

While Mac drives and the traffic becomes more and more chaotic, I am apt to relieve my tension by wriggling my toes. If this is not enough, I twist my ankles. Finally, if the stress is unbearable, and somehow it usually does become intolerable, I cross and recross my legs. I try not to say a word, but that does not mean I do not have plenty in mind!

How easy it is to fly six hundred miles an hour in the sky and not worry about bumping into another airplane, whereas driving thirty five miles an hour in this traffic, I am convinced we will be instantly killed.

One afternoon while meandering through the countryside, Mac says, hopefully, "You are going to snooze?"

"No, I think I'll follow the map," says Helen.

"Oh," says a disappointed Mac. He is growing tired of his back-seat driver.

Superhighway driving is a contest to see who will get there first. One passes everything slower, be that on a curve or in a tunnel or on the straightaway. Fast traffic always has the right of way and must use the left-hand lane. Should there be an accident involving a slow car in the fast lane, the slow car is at fault. By law the slow car must stay in the right-hand lane, unless it passes an even slower car. To pass a car the procedure is to drive directly behind the one ahead, blink headlights on and off and rev the motor several times. This is a signal saying, "move over!" It is incentive enough.

The variety of automobiles using the autostrada is intriguing. Everything from the tiny Fiats with little might to race car specimens like Ferraris with enormous vitality are apt to be traveling at the same time. Only motorcycles are not allowed on it. Fast traffic here means accelerating anywhere from 150 to 200 kilometers per hour, some one hundred twenty five miles per hour!

It is hard for me to enjoy taking a ride when the drive is so much jockeying for position around other vehicles. Mac says superhighway driving is a bore. I suppose the speeding and passing makes it more interesting on these beautifully engineered thoroughfares.

Two very small cars much in evidence are the Fiat 500, called the Cinque Cento and the Innocenti. Both look like little square boxes on wheels! For some reason, they always seem to be stuffed with people.

They remind me of the classical circus act: A small auto drives into the ring. Its door opens, and a dozen or more midgets pile out!

Perhaps because most of the Italian cars are little, they

seem to go faster than they actually do.

"The more noise, the less horsepower," says Mac.

During the sixties in the United States Mac drove a 124 Sport Fiat, painted a bright chartreuse green. It gave more pizzazz for less performance than any car of any other nation.

In three months we rent a total of six automobiles from Hertz, mostly Fiats. They are the most popular here. They are easy to drive and park and are reasonably comfortable. Most important of all, they are totally inconspicuous with so many like them in the potpourri of traffic.

Cars can be washed at a gas station. The car is usually driven to the rear of the lot where an attendant vacuums the inside and hoses off the outside, concentrating on the tires and windows. Next the car is moved over to the outdoor washing apparatus, called a lavatrice, and parked inside it. It is a good idea to set the emergency brake we learned when one time we forgot to set ours, and watched helplessly while the car started going ahead while in the washing process.

131

Luckily this was only a few inches, but the water pressure used is strong enough to move a car back and forth. Mounted on a steel framing, the lavatrice is composed of four huge rounded flexible brushes sitting upright and parallel to each other the exact width of an automobile plus one fat top roller brush. While a trickle of water flows onto them, they rotate scrubbing each side of the auto while a third brush runs over the top. This mechanism moves from the front to the back of the car and repeats itself in the opposite direction. The car is cleaned very well. When these finish, the brushes recede against the steel framing while a blower descends from above and literally blows off the excess water from the car, working backward, then forwards. When it finally returns to the front, the car is almost entirely dry and looks shiny clean. There is a wheel on the top of the blower which when it comes into contact with the car immediately lifts up thereby preventing any damage to the exterior of the car.

The only single problem is one cannot depend on which day these machines will be in service. In most stations this vital information is not posted.

☙

At many stations there is self service for fueling your car with gasoline. To accomplish this a ten thousand lira note is placed in a slot which then rolls the money inside the mechanism. This triggers the station's tank to release a specific amount of gasoline, which will pump into the fuel tank.

132

ༀ

We and dozens of others are queuing up at a toll gate to get onto the autostrada. We stack in reasonably neat, parallel rows. Out of the corner of my eye I see a car coming toward us at an angle totally out of sequence with everybody else. The driver is determined to break into our queue, picking the slot ahead of our bumper. Obviously he has no intention of taking his place at the end of the line where the rest of us had started. Mac sees this and turns our front wheels out toward the car, making it awkward to break in ahead of us.

I can see both what Mac is doing and what the other driver is trying to do. He has been thwarted by Mac. I see him mouthing words, which, thank heavens, I cannot hear. I hear all the words Mac is voicing, and that is enough. I want to laugh aloud at the two of them. Instead I concentrate on keeping my eyes straight ahead and my face dead-pan. Slowly we proceed to the toll gate with our crasher still waiting. Italians do not consider it etiquette to allow anyone to go ahead of them. Are we becoming Italian?

ༀ

Toll gates to the big autostrade can have the most unpretentious entrances to them. A sign pointing to the autostrada may direct traffic onto a small, windy country road carefully planted with all sorts of lush vegetation. Following it one suddenly turns the bend to be confronted by a toll gate. Here all traffic stops. The driver punches a red button and a ticket rolls out from a slot. This ticket will determine how much toll to pay when coming off the autostrada. If it is a tall truck going through the toll gate, there is on the right hand side of the gate a higher up red button to punch to collect the ticket. This saves the truck driver from having to personally get out of his truck in order to get his ticket thus holding up traffic from behind.

When coming off of the autostrada there is another line-up to pay toll. This time the ticket is handed to an attendant, who punches a machine to determine how many lira are owed. The amount shows up on a monitor directly ahead of the driver. Drivers try to pay and get through this process quickly so they can continue on to their destinations.

Ci vuole means it wants.

When using a gas station with an attendant, and he says, "How much?"

You could answer, "Ci vuole dieci galloni." I want ten gallons.

Sometimes you will hear an ex-Italian in America say, "She wants ten gallons."

Mac to Helen: "I'm glad you're sitting in the back seat. You might do that more often."

And I did and do. It is an excellent idea, a marvelous solution for riding tenseness. I would recommend it! Having the back of the front seat before me is the security I need to feel safe. From that day on I always sit directly behind the right·front seat. Both Mac and I like this arrangement although doormen are apt to find it quite strange.

By pushing the front seat all the way forward I have room to stretch my legs, and Mac has a convenient spot to put his maps. I use the rest of the back seat space for books and magazines. If the drive is making me nervous, I pick up a magazine and read, ignoring occurrences on the road. The interior of the Fiat is small enough so neither Mac nor I feel isolated from each other even with one of us sitting in the front and the other sitting in the back.

Happiness is wandering through the quiet countryside with both of us at ease and savoring the views.

౬

Suddenly an F-105 fighter airplane of the Italian air corps swoops over us. He flies low across the countryside and leaves a thundering echo as he passes. Where did it come from? He spoils the serenity of our afternoon.

౬

If you have the impression that man, standing in the grass beside the highway and staring at the distant hillsides, is contemplating the scenery, do take another look. Chances are he is relieving himself! Apparently nobody hides behind a bush here.

135

We are coming home from Firenze to the Poggio. Ahead of us is a mo-ped driver, a young man.

This particular section of the road is narrow and twisty with high walls of cut-stone on either side. Although it is paved, it is full of dips and bumps. There are numerous blind corners and no shoulders or sidewalks for pedestrians. Everybody drives fast. Mac concentrates on keeping our car in the right-hand lane to avoid oncoming traffic.

The young man is going fast. For a reason not apparent, he keeps looking back. Perhaps he wants to reassure himself that we are not too close. We are a distance of two or three car lengths behind. We watch him. I notice each time he turns to look, he looses balance, and his bike swerves. He quickly steadies himself, but it makes me jittery. I wish he would direct his attention on maneuvering and not on us.

He looks again. As he does, the front wheel of his bike hits the stone wall on the right side of the road. The young man looses control. He and the bike fall down on the pavement. He lands on his left shoulder and hits his unhelmeted head on the pavement. The bike is under him.

I gasp! Mac stops our car instantly. Nothing moves. Not a sound.

We watch horrified. Slowly, ever so slowly, the young man raises his head. He shakes it and sits up. He twists his body around and stands up. He feels his face. Looking down he sees his glasses lying on the pavement. He picks them up. They are bent but apparently unbroken. He puts them on.

Quickly he grabs his mo-ped and drags it to the side of the road. Mac and I breathe a sigh of relief.

The young man moves normally. Slowly Mac drives over to him as I roll down my window. "Are you ok?" we ask.

"Si," he nods to us.

He is calm and apparently unhurt. The bike is not broken. We slowly move on. As we do we note two people standing on the stone wall above observing. Down the road two other people have come out of the grocery store and are watching. No one says anything or offers help.

We arrive back at the Poggio feeling shaky. We are happy to be inside safe and sound. We thank God the young man is not severely injured.

⹃

These little mo-peds, or motorscooters as we know them, are driven everywhere. A person must be fourteen years old in order to use one, but no license is required. (Eighteen is the eligible age for an automobile license.) There is a mandatory law that anyone under sixteen years of age must wear a safety helmet when operating it. After that age it is optional whether the person wears one or not. It is thought since the bikes go so slowly, a helmet is not necessary for safety. Some of the little bikes go up to sixty or sixty five kilometers per hour. That is about forty miles per hour. They are not allowed on the autostrada.

⹃

While both men and women use mo-peds, it is most amusing to see young girls in their high heeled shoes, driving one. These little scooters are inexpensive to buy, faster than a bicycle, and easy to operate. Girls drive them everywhere, fearlessly weaving in and out and around on the heaviest trafficked streets. Sometimes they use hand signals, but more than likely do not. One never knows whether one will pass you on the right or left. Many a girl has a Gucci or Fendi handbag draped over her shoulder.

We learned the hard way mo-peds have parking spaces allotted especially for their own use. One day after much searching and not finding any space available for our car, we finally found an opening which is marked with several parallel stripes. With a flourish Mac maneuvers into it. An Italian man strolling by stopped, points to the stripes and says this spot is only for mo-peds. He shakes his head and states we will probably get a ticket if we stay. Although there are several other automobiles parked in similarly marked spaces, we elect to move our car. No sense fighting the bureaucracy.

We get back into the car and begin driving down a narrow street. After passing a series of parked cars we spot an opening. Mac pulls our car into position to maneuver it into a space. He is almost in the spot when he suddenly stops the car and yanks on the emergency brake. He gets out, leaving his door ajar.

"What are you doing?" I say, leaning out his door.

Mac is lifting a mo-ped from the upper half of the space and placing it directly in back of the car parked ahead. Now we will have room to get our own into the opening. I note it is a space for cars, not mo-peds. No stripes can be seen, but it is doubtful the mo-ped will get a ticket for using it.

℥

In all our driving we observe some young Italian women give the impression they are more the aggressors in a relationship than some of the men, inspite of any Italian masculine preferred syndrome!

℥

Since there are no shoulders on any roads it is important to keep brushing the roadsides so the vegetation does not grow into the lanes. There are highway crews who constantly man mowing machines to do this work. Usually two machines work in tandem, wonderful round discs at the end of steel booms which can be manipulated into any position or height to do the job. Their rotating blades chew up any type of brush touched and spread the debris back onto the ground for mulch. This clearing helps being able to see around corners too.

℥

Our sister-in-law, Clara, was riding with her husband along the autostrada. She noticed all the other cars were passing them. They were driving more than eighty miles an hour.

Her husband said he knew something was up when, fastening her seat belt, she said, "Come on, Henry, let's get going!"

From then on their driving was serious business.

§

There is a road from Mercatale to Panzano which was built by the Romans. It has likely been there for two thousand years. It is being replaced only now.

Imagine riding over the same paving stones, probably reinforced underneath with iron which was a part of the building code of that era on which Roman soldiers marched, dressed in their handsome armor! Gives one goosebumps to think about it.

Two thousand years is long before anyone tried to find a place called the United States of America.

§

"Mac, why do you suppose there is a kilometer sign marking off each kilometer to Siena?" Unusual to have each one marked.

"Somebody got the contract to do it, I imagine," answers Mac.

Driving along another finished highway, it suddenly stops and we are diverted onto a secondary road. Just as suddenly the highway begins again. The contractor for the unbuilt part probably had a dispute so any work completing the highway was abandoned.

❦

On a long drive from Lucca to Porto Ercole, we were detoured through a town called Vada. Vada is pronounced "Vah Dah" not "Vay Duh." Since we have a favorite aunt by that same name and immediately thought of her when we saw it here, we took a good look at the place.

It is an up and coming little community, pretty with seaside frontage and bustling with activity, especially from the traffic being routed through its center. Who knows what it may offer the tourist who stops to see. After much stopping and starting we are back on the highway again. For us this detour is a real inconvenience.

An enterprising place, this city called Vada. Must have a good chamber of commerce.

❦

With three or four cars and a bus coming directly toward us and a major road turning onto this two-lane highway, a car passes us at a high speed. We watch him pass another car as he approaches a blind curve.

Interesting to watch a semi-truck with a trailer in tow

hot-rod around another truck. He barely makes it back into line before a small Fiat, coming in the opposite direction, reaches him. But, then sometimes, small cars ride on the back fender of trucks and stay dangerously mid-center of the road waiting for traffic coming toward them to clear so they can pass and continue on.

The logic of highway driving is to get ahead and stay ahead of everyone else. Faster is better and such good sport.

&

"Look at that view from here!" Mac says looking left as we approach a right blind curve on the narrow road. Though he is in control of the car, and I know it, this not watching while visibility ahead is minimal worries me a lot.

&

Our friend Carol describes riding in an automobile with us another way. As Mac drives to Gaiole, winding along the twisty road filled with blind curves over the heights of the Chianti Mountains, she says excitedly, "Hoot, Mac, hoot!"

&

Mac had to learn to drive a European car so the back seat passenger is comfortable. On curved rural roads going too fast made the little car sway, causing the back seat passenger

142

considerable slipping and sliding in the seat even while wearing a seat-belt. Occasionally it made one dizzy. Mac finally understood when he experienced the slipping and sliding during a taxi ride while he was in the back seat. Each time we sped around a blind curve he would laugh, not because he thought it funny.

"Now you know how I feel," I told him. He did and quietly adjusted his own technique. Bless his sensitivity!

One day driving to Giovanna's we are surprised to see an amusement park set up nearby the stadium. It had not been there the day before. On the grounds are a half dozen or so glittering rides, the whirly kind which fascinate big and little children. Pitched directly in front of them is a fancy awning which shades several chairs around a table. People have gathered. The center of the group is an old woman. She has long braided hair and wears a flame red skirt. Its length almost covers her ankles. Standing beside her is a child dressed in shiny yellow satin.

No time to see more. The street light changes so we drive on. These people are gypsies. Maybe the old woman is a fortune teller! We assume they are a part of the retinue with the amusement park. It is the first time we have seen gypsies in Florence.

ॐ

Giovanna is giving me a hard time about pronunciation. In our class work we always recite aloud. When it is my turn, and usually I am first, she stops me continuously, making me look at her mouth as she says the word very loudly. I say it back to her as I hear it. She shakes her head.

"No, no, Mrs. Whiting. Listen to me. Can't you hear how it sounds?"

Truthfully I cannot. I had never seriously listened to Italian before these lessons so do not know how the language should sound. Her seriousness touches my funny bone. I almost giggle aloud. Giovanna, trying to make me hear, opens her mouth very wide, pronouncing the word in a loud, totally exaggerated way. She enunciates it distinctly, I guess, but I do not hear that. I am fascinated how she looks—all mouth and teeth. I completely miss the sounds.

ॐ

Good hindsight tells me how I should have been working with Giovanna. Because I have difficulty hearing the subtleties of its sounds, more reading aloud back and forth from the text to each other could have helped me a lot. If Giovanna had first read a paragraph, then asked me to reread the same one, she could have immediately pointed out my errors and helped correct them. I would have understood clearer perhaps being able to see the printed words as we read too. I was being asked to read without having the vaguest idea how Italian words should sound, look or be enunciated. No wonder the language was a puzzle for me.

On the other hand when Mac reads, she is all smiles. "Bellissimo, Mr. Whiting, you are sounding Italian!"

Precipitevolissimevolmente—although now obsolete, is the longest word in the Italian vocabulary. It means quickly.

Interested in hearing how it sounds I begin slowly pronouncing the word, syllable by syllable. Giovanna, who is correcting a paper Mac has prepared for his lesson, impatiently finishes with me, saying "-volmente" as I do. She continues working on the paper without looking up.

Then Mac says, softly, "precipitevolissimevolmente."

"Bellissimo!" says Giovanna, looking up. "Mrs. Whiting, he has such a talent. It is so special. Bravo, Mr. Whiting!"

"Mac always does things well, Giovanna," I say, slightly miffed. My own spirits are sagging and in need of a little encouragement too.

Terminato and finito are two other words whose meanings fascinate us. Both mean stop or finished.

Both are understood best when used referring to eating. Terminato means finished, but leaving some food on the plate. Basically, it means I have stopped eating. Another example is with reading a book. Terminato would mean you put the book aside for a while, but it is not entirely read.

Finito on the other hand means in the case of food, there is no more on the plate. It is all gone. In the book example it means it has been totally read.

These subtleties in the language, and there are many, make it interesting to study.

Mac asks Giovanna to help him learn to decipher the daily newspaper. The grammar and vocabulary differs somewhat from the academic reading he has been doing. We miss not knowing the daily news. Stories from the newspaper are definitely more interesting than translations from Dante's wanderings through the Inferno. Giovanna does not think newspaper writing proper Italian for her student, but she is a good sport and agrees to help.

A translation by Mac:

Schiacciato da un Palo—Crushed by a pole.

San Casciano—There was a serious accident at work last Monday in San Casciano. It took the life of Salvatore Capone, twenty six years old, born in S. Cipriano di Aversa (Ce) and now of Figline Valdarno.

The misfortune happened while Salvatore, who worked for the firm of his father-in-law, was operating a bulldozer to move a large pilaster.

To avoid the stump of an olive tree, the young man was forced to carry out a hazardous maneuver which together with the slope of the terrain caused the huge pilaster to slip out of the control of the machine. The pilaster tumbling backwards rolled completely over Salvatore, shifting him a few meters and caving in his chest.

This story probably proves Giovanna's point. It is typical of the news in the daily newspaper.

ℰ

One afternoon a truck drives up to the Poggio, comes through the gate, and unceremoniously dumps a huge load of cut stone onto the side of the driveway. There are slabs of rock, some sizable, lying in one big heap. A few break apart as they fall, making little coves. We do not know where all this is to be used.

That evening during our dinner Mac has an overseas telephone call. When he goes on talking for some time, I

149

leave the dining room table and wander into the kitchen. Dilia is washing dishes and giggling to herself. She beckons to me. Together we look out the window.

Massimo has discovered the stone pile. He has made one of the coves into a house. Around it are piles of his cars. His bed pillow is inside. Massimo has squeezed himself into the cove too. There he is, the picture of contentment, lying on his pillow, playing with a car. Dilia and I smile at each other.

All week long Massimo plays in his house. He never wants to come out. His parents have difficulty getting him to bed. Massimo does not bother anyone. Massimo's Casa, we call it.

❧

Mac and I are away for the weekend. The first thing we notice when we come back is Massimo's Casa is gone! All the rocks are neatly in a pile. No sign of Massimo's pillow or cars.

"Dilia, where is Massimo's Casa?" we both inquire.

"No more. Basta." she replies and offers no explanation.

Around the corner comes Massimo in high gear. He careens across the terrace on his bicycle. The cat scoots hastily aside. Mac is nearly bumped. Our Massimo, pre-casa, his high-powered energy is flying in all directions. He is loudmouthed and deliberately bothering everyone.

❧

Apparently Sante felt the pile of rocks a dangerous place for Massimo to play. They might shift and hurt him.

150

Although we do agree, we are so sorry he has to loose his casa. Now Massimo does not have any special spot where he can be by himself.

In their apartment Massimo shares his parents' bedroom —and bed. It never occurs to Dilia or Sante that he would be a more contented child if he slept alone. We suspect Dilia does not want to give up her baby.

We think all children, but especially this little boy, need a special place to dream and play, but most of all, be at peace with themselves.

The liquor store in Impruneta is run by a handsome old woman with an unusually high squeaky voice. We have never heard anyone talk at such a high pitch as she. She sells us wine so many times she recognizes us when we come into her store.

Mac loves to tease her. When he buys vodka or rum, he asks if she has anything stronger. She always tells him if he buys anything stronger it will burn out his stomach.

Burning his stomach while drinking her liquor tickles her funnybones. She guffaws so hard, her whole face crinkles into a mass of wrinkles. All you can see are her teeth which are huge in size as her gums have receded.

She is a smart merchant, a person with great integrity. She knows if we overindulge, we will cease being her good customers. She does not want that to happen. We like and respect her.

No one of culture in Tuscany drinks only wine at a meal. Wine is accompanied by an equal volume of water. We do not see people under the influence of too much liquor. There are no red noses or puffy-eyed citizens here.

Dilia answered the telephone saying, "Hello?"
Mac teases her about using English instead of Italian. Dilia says she does not know how to talk anymore. Should she use Italian or English or maybe French talking with us?

What we admire so much about Dilia is her willingness to try something new. She does it with good spirits, genuine enthusiasm and a very much in-charge attitude. Not everybody can approach new situations with such confidence and serenity.

It is raining—again. The sky is completely gray. There is not a sign of life that I can see from my windows in the Pigeon's Roost. It thunders and lightnings and more rain falls. A dismal afternoon.

All the rye which was planted under the olive trees is cut. It waits to be raked or plowed under. This rain is going to make it rot. The olive trees are blooming. The fruit will then form. This year's olive crop is expected to be good.

The grape crop and all the other fruits have had too much water. None of it is picked. It has grown unusually large, but is not ripening due to the lack of sunshine.

We have had about four days of sun since we first arrived in early April. It is now the end of June. What a disappointment to us. So very few days of warm sunshine to loll around outdoors with the flowers and the lovely views.

Springtime is not sun-time this year.

Today Massimo shows us he can turn a somersault. We clap our hands and tell him that is fine. He turns another, and we clap again. He tries one on the concrete terrace. What a grimace! That hurt.

He goes back to the grass and turns a super-duper big one. Then he runs off around the corner of the Poggio. We have to smile at his showmanship.

Our daughters, Helen and Mary, decide to pick out a pair of earrings for Dilia. These are to be their special thank you to Dilia for all she did that made their visit to the Poggio especially pleasant. They spend many fun hours choosing from huge assortments in shops on the Ponte Vecchio. They finally select oval dangle earrings of dark red coral set in gold. They are pretty.

Dilia is thrilled. She puts them on immediately. The girls are so pleased. Both Helen and Mary tell Dilia many times how nice the earrings look.

Several weeks later after the girls go back to the United States, Dilia is still wearing their earrings. I believe she has worn them every single day since they gave them to her.

❦

There are two spaniel dogs in our neighborhood whom we call Old Dogs Tray after the nursery rhyme about the friendly "Old Dog Tray."

In fact, these are unfriendly. They are quite ferocious until paid the least bit of attention. At that point their tails wag. They lie down rolling over on their backs wanting to have their stomachs rubbed.

That is today. Next morning as the jogger goes by, they growl and act ferocious again. Making friends must start all over.

❦

The quiet of the afternoon is suddenly broken by the peal of church bells in Pozzolatico. A funeral is in progress. Say a prayer.

⚜

In Italy the government owns all the church buildings. We had thought the Vatican did. The Vatican is responsible only for what goes on inside those buildings. All arredi sacri, movable possessions, inside the building belong to the priest. The church as an entity does not own anything. It has the use of the real estate, and this real estate belongs to the government! When the priest dies, the arredi sacri is willed to the next priest.

Confusing? Yes, it is.

⚜

Walking onto the terrace by the driveway gate to enjoy fresh air and a sliver of sunshine, I notice one of the cats sitting by the driveway gate. It is meowing. It is unusual to see one of the cats sitting so still and meowing so loudly.

I walk over to it. Poor thing! It is in a cardboard box. There is a string tied around its neck and fastened to the box. The string is tight, so tight the cat cannot move. Had it tried the cat might have broken its neck.

I sense how this happened and who is probably responsible. To assure that this never takes place again, I decide to be very calm in case little eyes are observing. I quietly call Dilia. When she comes out of the house, I point to the cat. She understands immediately and unties the miserable thing. It shakes itself and runs off into the bushes.

Overly energetic little boys need constructive things to do.

"Drink an egg!" she says.

"What? Are you serious, Giovanna?"

She is. One cracks a fresh, raw egg into a cup. Add to it a few drops of lemon juice. A little salt and pepper too. Stir this well and drink! Giovanna claims this good for one's health and well being.

Mamma mia!

Massimo takes off his calf-length, yellow, rubber boots to show us his new socks. They are maroon color, ankle-length for summer. He is so proud of them he runs all over the terrace in his maroon stocking feet. He stops. Turning a big somersault on the grass, he disappears around the corner. The big clown!

Dilia has enrolled Massimo in swimming class. The scuolabus will pick him up at the Poggio and deliver him back when the class finishes.

We are happy he has something special to do. He needs to be with children his own age.

After much deliberation I have decided to call a halt to my Italian lessons. Two months plus into them my tongue is sore, my brain is tired, and I am having continuing nightmares about what we are studying. That is ridiculous, I know. I cannot seem to assimilate what I have learned into any comprehension of what someone says to me. That seems just beyond my grasp. A frustrating situation! Maybe I need to do my learning in a less rushed and less scholastic manner. Simply talking about ordinary things would help me "hear." I am not absorbing enough from these lessons of conjugating irregular verbs, writing sentences, and always doing everything speedily to be onto the next lesson. I cannot remember from one lesson to the next. They all jumble together and for me do not have any relationship to simply conversing in Italian. The gist of this is too difficult to explain to Giovanna. Hope she will understand. I do not want to hurt her feelings.

Today I am sitting on the terrace, wrapped in a snugly blanket, but luxuriating in some warmish sunshine. Finally we have a sunny afternoon! Mac has gone into Florence for his Italian lesson. He will continue without me. Around the corner of the Poggio comes Dilia. Hesitatingly, in Italian, she asks me if I would like to . . . I do not quite understand what she is asking. She beckons me into the kitchen. Using the dizionario-italiano, she points to the word "to visit." She turns to another word: "house." Oh! She is inviting me to her house! I am totally surprised. I tell her I would love to visit her casa and am so pleased to be asked. In all the time we have been here neither Mac nor I have ever been inside her home.

℥

We go through our mutual laundry to her door. Down two flights of stairs we enter her kitchen-dining room.

The place is neat as a pin. Lots of sunshine comes in the window. To one side of the room are the doors of two bedrooms. One of these has a huge king-size bed. The other is empty.

"Whose room is this, Dilia?" I ask.

"Oh, this room is no good." she replies. "Too cold and damp. We don't use it." I realize this might be Massimo's bedroom. He is such a big boy to be in the same bed with his parents, even if this is the Italian custom.

I sit down at their dining room table while Dilia brews us a cup of espresso. I enjoy being here. We discuss her crocheting. She has made doilies to go under her numerous flower pots and the bowl on the table. They are beautifully done in a turquoise thread with a fine crochet hook.

What a talented person Dilia is! Every part of her home reflects this.

℥

I start knitting an afghan throw with an intricate, complicated hundred stitch repeat pattern across and a twenty six row repeat down. I use a fine, cobwebby one-ply yarn,

158

which has to be rolled into balls before any work could begin. It is a lovely feeling, having knitting needles in my hands and yarn passing through my fingers. I must concentrate hard for each new row needs to be counted to be correct. This work is a substitute for my Italian lessons. For me it is more stimulating and infinitely more satisfying. Giovanna is fascinated with development of the afghan. She does not knit. Every so often when she gives Mac writing to do, she comes over to watch me work. She kneels down in front of my chair, takes the finished part in her two hands and murmurs, "Bello, molto bello, Mrs. Whiting." "Beautiful, very beautiful, Mrs. Whiting."

One afternoon at Giovanna's apartment I am peacefully knitting while Mac is having his lesson. The window is open, and I am breathing the crisp, fresh air of spring with enjoyment. Suddenly, I hear a male voice outside coming from a loud speaker. I cannot tell whether he is announcing the beginning of a political rally or advertising something to sell.

The noise interrupts Mac and Giovanna. They stop the lesson. We all listen, hear shouting, but cannot make out the words. We wait until the truck is nearer to the apartment. All three of us stick our heads out the window as do many others in the neighborhood. We see a large truck moving down the street. Using his loudspeaker the driver is announcing to everybody he has fresh potatoes for sale!

Shortly before we are to leave the Poggio, Dilia calls me into the kitchen. She hands me a package, beautifully wrapped in colored paper. I look at her quizzically, and she tells me in Italian it is a present for Mac and me.

I am excited and call Mac. Together we open the box and find an Italian espresso pot inside. It is identical to the one she has been using for us these past months. We are moved by the sentimentality of this gift. We say so in rapid English. She understands. She says she wants us to have proper coffee when we are at home.

Then in Italian Dilia proceeds to tell us exactly how to make coffee with this pot. We tell her we will think of her each time we use it and hope our espresso will be as good as hers.

Mac has felt in the best of health these past months. Free of allergy attacks since we have lived here. No corn or corn products, no peanuts, no garlic powder in the superb cuisine. In the soft air no allergens challenge him with sinus pain, bleary eyes, flashes of rage and spells of dozing. He feels like he has gone to Heaven. This will have much consideration in our returning. Perhaps we should come to the Poggio another season?

Certamente!

Our rental time ends at the Poggio, and we move into a hotel in Florence. We still need to pick up laundry that Dilia had not finished and a few other personal things at the Poggio. When the laundry is ready, Dilia telephones and at the same time invites us for dinner. We accept with pleasure.

~

We arrive at the Poggio to find it a forlorn place. It is totally locked with windows shuttered, curtains drawn. It is so dark we think it looks sad. Of course, we know better. Dilia has cleaned and polished in anticipation of our visit. The good Italian housekeeper she is always leaving cleaned rooms in total darkness. We giggle. The atmosphere is just like it was living here. We pull back the curtains and throw open the shutters to let in the warm evening air. Tonight there is a spectacular sunset of pink and rose against a gray sky. Then we hear the familiar voice saying, "Pronto, signori!" We know our dinner is ready to be served.

~

We walk into the dining room. Dilia has outdone herself. The table with a red cloth has our two familiar places set with the usual two plates, one on top of the other, fork, knife and two glasses. The bottle of water is open. A special bottle of Chianti is ready to pour. Dilia brings in a platter of grilled chicken with lots of fresh rosemary from the Poggio berms. She has our favorite vegetables, bietole, beet greens, and baby

161

peas from her own garden, and to tease Mac, who claims he never will eat it, a bit of zucchini.

ℰ

We eat with total enjoyment. To Mac's amused annoyance il gatto and la gatta run in and out of the dining room. It is finally warm enough so doors are left open. The cats, smelling wonderful odors, come in to investigate. Each time one appears, Mac flaps his napkin and hisses at it which makes the cat scoot around the corner barely out of sight. As soon as Mac stops flapping and hissing, the other comes in. I laugh. It is comical to watch.

Dilia, happy to have us, hovers around. She tells us how much they all miss us. We tell her we miss them too. She wants to know if everything is all right. Are we being well treated at that hotel? We reassure her they do a good job, but it is not like being here with her.

At the end of the meal when we think we can hardly get up, Dilia produces her special dolce. It is a marvelous apple tart with a crust thin and crispy. It melts in our mouth. We are so touched she made this especially for us. "No, Dilia, we cannot eat any more. Not even one tiny little piece!" She would have been thrilled if we had consumed the entire dolce! We ask her to serve coffee on the terrace so we can watch the gorgeous sunset.

ℰ

162

We sit on the terrace wall with our tiny cups of espresso. We observe the blooming rosebushes so pretty in this light. Their perfume is delicious. We feel great nostalgia for this place. We each gaze at the various vistas we have so enjoyed. We can see the neighboring villas, tiny Pozzolatico with its church steeple, the beautiful olive groves, the distant Certosa with its imposing architecture, our neighbors' homes. I look at Mac, and he looks back at me. We finish our coffee. It is time to leave, really leave. It may be a long time before we return.

Back into the house we collect our things, my purse, the laundry which is neatly folded for Mac, and a couple of knickknacks. After one last long and final review of the Poggio we walk out to the car.

꒰

There are the three Casinis, Dilia, Sante, and Massimo, waiting to say a final goodbye.

I shake hands with Sante, and say, "Arrivederci, Sante!"

He shakes my hand and with a big smile says, "Please come back soon!"

I throw my arms around Dilia and kissed her on both cheeks. She kisses me with tears in her eyes. I have tears in mine too.

I rumple Massimo's hair and remind him to be a good boy and not tease i gatti, the cats!

Mac shakes hands with them all and says his goodbyes in proper Italian.

We get into our car. Backing out onto via di Riboia with

Sante watching for oncoming traffic, Dilia is standing by the gate, and Massimo, quiet for once, is in the middle of the driveway. We wave one more time. Down the road we go.

Slowly, slowly we drive back to Firenze. Each curve brings special vistas and memories. The evening sky is now a deep rosy pink with a misty opalescent gray background. The olive groves are a silvery green and shimmer in this light. There is no breeze, just the ever deepening colors and warmth of the oncoming night.

We promise each other to return soon.

PART
2

A Poem

I'm Nobody! Who are you?
Are you - Nobody - Too?
Then there's a pair of us?
Don't tell! they'd advertise - you know!

How dreary - to be - Somebody!
How public - like a Frog -
To tell one's name - the livelong June -
To an admiring Bog!

Emily Dickinson
c. 1861

2ND PROLOGUE

Mac and I get on the elevator to ride up to the restaurant on the roof. With us is an elegant looking older couple. She is blonde, stylish, poised. He is short, bald, spritely.

"Buon giorno!" we greet them.

They look at us and, with a distinct American accent, together say, "Good morning!"

We talk to each other quietly as the man turns to his wife. "They are speaking English!" he says excitedly to her. He turns to us. "You do speak English?"

We nod. He smiles impishly. "I can't understand a thing these Italians say so I just raise my eyebrows and wink at

169

them!" Laughing, he winks at us.

The elevator door opens. I stand aside, allowing the lady to precede me.

"Apres vous," she says to me, not remembering her husband had just learned we understand English.

Americans . . . he, happy, carefree, enjoying himself, while she, sophisticated, but slightly disoriented, is not as confident. How adjusted we have become!

They think we are Italian!

We are living in Florence now, staying at the Excelsior Hotel. It feels like a breath of fresh air to be in a cosmopolitan city after three months of country life. Here there is noise and activity and the marvelous Arno river flowing outside our front windows. We overlook a parking lot on the other side, providing a constant source of comings and goings. With the push of a button we call Estelle, the daily housekeeper, or one of several floor waiters who bring food or drinks. When someone knocks at our door, we answer, "avanti!" and in they come with huge smiles, anxious to satisfy any need. Often they ask about our family and love seeing any photographs we have with us. They praise our Italian. We truly feel relaxed, well cared for—in charge.

The Excelsior in Florence has a whole network of personnel who make this hotel hum. One's first introduction to its atmosphere is with the doormen, who greet you with smiles as you drive up to the entrance. The day we arrive, the doorman on duty is wearing a brand-new hat, an impressive high crowned affair with a shiny visor. We remark how handsome it is. He starts a long spiel agreeing it is and removes it from his head so we can admire it as we talk. Together we agree it seems a bit heavy to use. He calls the porters, who nod at us, then look somewhat skeptically at the twenty plus pieces of assorted luggage we need toted. Even though the cases are small in size, there still are twenty pieces to be carried and accounted for upstairs. Silently they arrange every one on racks and whisk them away.

We go through the revolving door and turn left. There is the reception desk with the reservation managers. Since we have stayed here previously and are remembered, we are welcomed back with handshakes and told our suite, numbered due tre quattro (234), is waiting for us. We have the feeling it has been empty all the time we were away and simply awaiting our return. Not true, of course.

We cross over to the other side of the large lobby to be greeted with smiles and handshakes by the concierges, all four of them! How glad they are to see us! How long will we be staying?

We look over to the right corner of the lobby. The elderly European woman is there as we hoped she might be—the oldest permanent resident in the hotel. She chose this place as her retirement home and rents a suite of rooms for herself and her nurse. She sits in this corner before and after she has luncheon. She walks with a cane as she fell in one of the dining rooms and broke her hip several months ago. One would never guess she had such an injury so bright and alert she is. Every noon she has a meal in the dining room. Once we had a long conversation when we were seated next to her table. What a lively ninety-year-old she is with a keen mind, full of a multitude of interests from a long, satisfying life. We wave. She recognizes us and nods.

We are friends with the waiters in the restaurants as we usually lunch in one or another. The two headwaiters always teasingly greet Mac by saying, "Yes, Signore, I know what you order: salsiccia, insalata verde, pane di compagna, e vino bianco Antinori—sausage, green salad, country bread and white Antinori wine. E una bottiglia San Pellegrino, and a bottle of San Pellegrino water. Si, una grande bottiglia! Yes, a large bottle! Wouldn't you like to try something different today, Signor Whiting?"

Mac knows the girls in the telex office rather well as he is forever sending messages whereas I enjoy the ministrations of Fabrizio and his staff in the beauty salon. What a talent with the scissors!

It is an interesting group of people who come from all the surrounding areas of Florence to work here. We have never been in another hotel where the teamwork is as good as this one. A pleasure to be their guests.

☙

The hotel porter said to me, "All Americans say ok. All your movie stars say ok. You ask an American a question, and he answers you ok. Now you say ok to me. Can't Americans say anything else?"

☙

Fred! How good to see you."

One day in front of the hotel I spy Frederick Hand, our wonderful driver/guide. He is standing beside his limousine. How long ago was it he first drove us all over the city, patiently explaining the sites? Now we are old friends. We like to catch up on his doings whenever we see him.

"Hello, Madame!" he greets me, shaking my hand and bussing me on both cheeks, Italian style.

"How's Sor?"

"Wonderfully well, Fred. And Mrs. Hand? How is she?"

"Oh, the ole girl's the same—still enjoying retirement. You know, they'se gave her her typewriter when she retired, Madame? Nice of themse to do that."

"Yes, that certainly was nice." Fred has told me this story before. "Here comes Mac."

"Hello, Fred," says Mac, joining us and extending his hand. "How's everything? You look so good. You're driving someone, Fred?"

"Oh, yas, Sor, Madame. They'se sent me to Leghorn this

174

morning." (The English refer to the city of Livorno as "Leghorn". We cannot understand how they can possibly translate Livorno to "Leghorn"!) "To meet the cruise ship, y'know, Sor. Gets in at four thirty in the morning! Well, as I'se speaks English, they'se gave me these two ole girls. Americans, y'know, Sor. Wall, the two ole dears, they'se wanted t'see Florence. So I'se drove them hare. Now its nine thirty in morning. We'se driven in from Leghorn. That takes a while, over an hour, y'know. Already we'se been to the Domo and the Pitti Palace, Sor, Madame."

Fred sighs as we digest this information.

Then I say, "But where are they now, Fred?" I am wondering what sort of harridans these two females must be.

"They'se in thar eating, Madame," says Fred, pointing to the entrance of the Excelsior. Another pause and a deep sigh.

"Do y'know, Sor, Madame, what they'se said to me? They'se said, that is the livelier one of the two, said, and she talks all the time. She turned t'me, and she's said, 'Fred, you do speak such good English. You speak awfully good English for an Italian!' And, hare I am an Englishman even tho' I'se lived hare 'most t'past forty yars, right hare in It-tal-lee, that is. Honestly, Sor, Madame!" He is indignant so his speech seems even more English-English than usual.

Our concierge tells us some Arabs are staying at the hotel. They request an English driver. The hotel assigns Freddie Hand and tells them Fred has been imported from England exclusively for their specific use. They believe this and are flattered.

Ah, the Italian culture succeeds again!

⟨ఄ⟩

A waiter in the hotel dining room is speaking with two women guests. I hear him say he can speak both French and English.

"Mac, "I understood what that waiter said."

Mac looks at me and says, "You should. He is speaking Italian."

I laugh because I am getting to the point of not knowing whether I am hearing Italian, French or English. German I do recognize.

⟨ఄ⟩

Sitting at our table in the garden restaurant on top of our hotel, we have a marvelous view of the rooftops of Florence. They are fascinating, like no other in any city in the world— except, perhaps, Budapest. Florence is surrounded by hills which display outlines of villas against the sky. How does it happen the core of the city is the commercial section and stays in the center of the city while residences fan out from it undisturbed by commercialism?

This city is unique!

⟨ఄ⟩

There is nothing more nouveau riche than having a new tile roof. Everyone apologizes for his unless it is at least two hundred years old.

$$\mathfrak{E}$$

This day we go directly to the buffet table before enjoying the view. Two handsome prosciutto hams sit in holders waiting to be carved. Delicious looking. I do a double take and suddenly loose my appetite. One ham is complete with fur still on its hoof! I persuade Mac to eat elsewhere.

$$\mathfrak{E}$$

Just for fun I decide to write down some common Italian proper names. I realize I am not familiar with any. A man might be Marcello, Bruno, Tiziano, Rolando, Alberto, Guido, Sandro, Nicolo, or Luigi. Perhaps a woman is Flavia, Paola, Lucia, Donatella, Vittoria, Fiamma, Laura, or Alessandra. Giovanna tells me her name translates to Joan in English, but somehow our Giovanna does not seem like a Joan to us.

$$\mathfrak{E}$$

I was given five hundred lira for change yesterday, a coin. I like the feel of coins and always look at them. This is an interesting piece. It is minted of two metals, and it has Braille along its rim. I ask and am told the Braille is an innovation here in Italy. A few Scandinavian countries and The Netherlands use it on some of their paper money. What a boon for the blind this must be.

♧

J.R. of the TV series, Dallas, is broadly smiling at us from a billboard. "Io scelgo perche non attacca ai denti!" he says holding a package of Happydent Brooklyn in his hand. He wears his huge white cowboy hat and looks very American. Dallas is one of the most popular TV series in Italy.

Driving by I get the impression with such a broad smile he is advertising toothpaste, but we find out Happydent is chewing gum. Translated he is saying, "I choose Happydent because it does not stick to the teeth!"

♧

The leg of the desk in our room is loose. This desk is an antique with deeply bowed legs, the type known in the furniture trade as gambe. It is not a convenient size to use as it is too narrow for writing comfortably. It is too handsome a piece of furniture to be in a hotel room. Mac is concerned because the desk seems to be extremely shaky. He decides to do something about having it fixed. A repairman comes one afternoon in the middle of Mac's Italian lesson. He will continue these as long as we stay in Italy. We persuade Giovanna to teach in our rooms in the Excelsior instead of our traveling to her home on Carnesecche. She is most agreeable to this new plan.

He and Giovanna watch the repairman take out of his toolbox a piece of metal about four inches long and a quarter inch thick. He gets out sticky tape. He sits down on the carpet. He places the metal against the damaged spot on the leg. With the tape he wraps the metal onto the leg, securing it tightly.

"He's produced a splint!" I exclaim, walking in and observing the result.

"It's better than me bumping into it and having the whole desk crash to the floor," asserts Mac.

What a strange sight seeing a desk with a bandage.

๕

A literal translation from La Nazione, a national Italian newspaper by Mac:

Michele Zaza (Crazy Mike) 39 year old boss of the anti-Cutolo Camorra faction and liason between this new family and the Sicilian-American Mafia has wound up in handcuffs again (for the fifth time in three years) after having disappeared on the evening of December 29 from the luxury clinic in Rome in which he had been held.

He was captured in Paris with his lieutenant, Nunzio Barbarossa, owner of shops, night clubs and pizzerias, and also wanted for some time.

With Crazy Mike was his wife, Anna Maria Liguori, 35 years old, just returned from Los Angeles, where she owns a million dollar home in Beverly Hills.

When criminalpol agents, with some from the Paris anti-drug squad, took him just in front of the elegant gate to the palatial home of Nunzio Barbarossa where he had been hidden. The Boss admitted to being Michele Zaza, then he lost control and broke a window in the car which he was made to get into, "with bracelets" on his wrists. At the police station, where they found on him French identity papers and a huge sum of money, Zaza used the old gimmick of his ailment (he is known to be suffering from mitralic stenosis, having been operated on in Houston by cardiac surgeon de Bakey, and wearing a pace-maker), which served him well another time: in fact he is now a patient, under guard, in the hospital de L'Hotel Dieu.

The hunt began right after the notorious escape of December 29th, the investigators concurred in the finding that "Crazy Mike" headed straight for foreign soil. It was necessary then to keep an eye on his family, who were in the capitol at a residence on Piazza di Vigna Stelluti.

Telephone bugs and tails were set up. Everyday Zaza telephoned his wife (daughter of that Guiseppe Liguori taken in the "blitz" of February 4, 1983), taking only two and a half minutes. One day his wife also dropped out of sight. The children stayed in Rome with the baby-sitter. The attentions of the sleuths concentrated on her.

℃

Saturday nights we have unplanned entertainment from our balcony. It is a female impersonator who performs in the parking lot. She is tall, very thin, has long black straight hair, wears dark red lipstick and extremely high heel shoes. Her dresses are satin sheaths with slits. She saunters around the parking lot, shaking her hair back and forth as she tosses her head from side to side, trying to get attention. Sometimes she brings her friend who is shy and mostly sits in their automobile, a brand-new BMW. They cause traffic jams and general confusion. Drivers cannot believe what they see as they circle around the corner and come face to face with these two. The taller one likes to lean on a driver's windowsill and carry on conversations with the passengers inside the car. Occasionally she gets into a car and drives around the block. Sometimes she totally ignores everybody and sits on the hood of a parked car, swinging a leg back and forth while studying her fingernails. This causes much hilarity and chaos with the traffic.

One day as we are walking back to the hotel, we see her getting out of a car with a girl. It is obvious she is a he, and he is dressed as a man not as a woman. He is the same tall, very thin person we watch Saturday evenings strutting around the parking lot. We stare and are not absolutely sure whether he looks better in slacks and shirt or in a white satin sheath, cut very low in front and skirt slit high showing a lot of leg.

ঙ

A pink slip of paper dropped from an automobile as it sped down the street:

"Mercoledi 23 Giugno

SCIOPERO GENERALE REGIONALE DI TUTTE LE
CATEGORIE PER L'INTERA GIORNATA"

And on the pillow of the bed in our hotel room a white
slip of paper:

"WE ARE SORRY TO INFORM YOU THAT
TOMORROW 23ND JUNE THERE WILL BE A GENERAL
STRIKE IN OUR REGION AND THEREFORE SHORT-
COMINGS WILL OCCUR IN OUR SERVICES, ETC."

And so when we awake late this morning the corridor
outside our room is quiet. Not a sound of any of the service
people moving about. An unusual happening because they
are noisy morning people. Immediately we realize the strike
is on.

⚘

Nothing is open in the city during the time of the strike,
certainly no store. Small restaurants may give some service
by their owner, but there are no waiters. Buses and taxis stop
as well. Sad to see a tour bus from another country drive up,
and a group of people get off at our hotel—all expecting a
nicely served breakfast. Of course there is none. The dining
room is closed. The waiters are on strike as well as all the
kitchen help. Only a single concierge is in service at the front
desk in the lobby. Any other work in the entire hotel is
suspended.

᭶

After completing the specified number of striking hours, the marching finishes, and all speeches have been delivered. Everything starts up again. Everybody has done the sciopero so they all come back to work. It is exactly as if nothing out the ordinary had ever happened.

᭶

While this goes on, Mac dresses and walks out to find an open bar. Italians must have their espresso even during a crisis like a strike. He returns with espresso in paper cups and marvelous powdered sugar doughnuts. Never did a breakfast taste so good. With such a wonderful treat we do not mind the sciopero at all.

᭶

"Avanti! Buona sera," I say to our room waiter. "Per favore, di ghiaccio e le limone 'slices' . . . Come si dice 'slice'?" Come in! Good evening. Please how do you say "slice"? Fetta? OK. "Oh, e anche due bottiglie di San Pellegrino, grande, e due bottiglie tonica. Grazie." Oh, and also two bottles of San Pellegrino, large, and two bottles of tonic. Thank you.

My Italian, improving enough to order an evening cocktail, although hardly academic. The waiter brought everything, including a whole lemon! My word for slices apparently is incorrect.

❧

"Che tempo fa?" What is the weather like? "Fa bel tempo." The weather is beautiful. Our nightly television weather report. "A tutti, buona sera," starts the friendly weatherman. "To all a good evening!" This weatherman is no NBC Willard wearing a funny hat, huge boutonniere, and toupee. Ours has steel gray hair, dresses conservatively and wears quite ordinary steel rimmed glasses. He proceeds with a comprehensive report, using maps with numbers and symbols—A and B to denote highs and lows of the current weather pattern. We hear words like variable or poco nuvoloso which mean changeable or perhaps partly cloudy with a little unpleasantness. Mistakes occur. A thunderstorm strikes that is explained as a surprise from the north. Night after night we start our evenings listening to this. Italian is easier to understand when you are certain of the context.

❧

Interesting to note—housewives on television commercials are always brunettes, never blondes or redheads! Men on television are never either blonde or redhead, but are brunette or silver maned. Women television reporters are very stylishly clothed in handsome blouses and wear enormous clear plastic or horn rimmed glasses. Mostly they are blondes, occasionally redheads, but hardly ever brunettes. This seems atypical as most every woman we see here appears to be brunette.

ऍ

One noon we are lunching at the roof restaurant after a morning of sightseeing. We are lulled by the view of the Arno and enjoy resting our feet. Suddenly we notice a small automobile driving along the opposite river bank. This is most unusual. The driver stops the car almost under the bridge, gets out and walks around to open the trunk. He pulls something out, placing it on the ground. He returns to the car and takes out a long narrow board. Next he strips off his trousers, throws them in the trunk and close the hatch. He walks over to the thing on the ground and attaches something to it. We cannot see each detail as we are too far away, but he has our attention, as well as some of the waiters who begin hovering around our table. All of us wonder what he is doing.

Suddenly the thing on the ground takes a shape. The man has inflated a rubber craft—a kayak! He drags it to the river's edge, placing it very gently in the water. He is holding a long board, obviously an oar. He carefully climbs into the boat, positioning himself in dead center. He looks very oversized in a very undersized vessel. Now the maitre d' has joined the waiters along with Mac and I watching this undertaking. The current of the river is strong. We all wonder aloud what he can be thinking of rowing a small craft like this across it.

Row he does, straight across the Arno. He seems not to be the slightest dismayed by the current or by the fact not too far from him the Arno river becomes a huge waterfall making it drop substantially several feet lower. When he reaches our bank, he turns the kayak around and proceeds to row back to the other side. Once there he beaches the boat, gets out, and pulls it onto the bank. He lets the air out, carefully rolls it up and replaces it in the trunk. He puts in the oar, takes out his trousers, and closes the trunk. Pulling on his pants he climbs into the car. Off he drives down the river bank and up onto the highway. We all watch with open mouths. As one we shout "bravo!" and shake our heads almost unbelieving what we have just seen. What an exercise! Perhaps some friend had dared him to try.

We come back to our room after lunch, tired and ready to take a nap. There is a car horn blowing in the parking lot directly below us. We pay little attention to this and go into the bedroom to sleep. In the distance we can still hear the horn.

"Hope that isn't going to go on all afternoon," I say to Mac, promptly close my eyes and am asleep.

Two hours pass. I awake, dress and walk into our other room. The car horn is still blowing. I look out the window to see if I can tell which one it is. There are many cars in the lot, but one has its parking lights on even though there is sunlight. "That's the horn-blower, I bet," I say aloud.

The tooting goes on and off, on and off, on and off. I time

The flowers the Italians love best.

Roses grow everywhere . . . their blossoms are enormous.

Square at Greve.

Loggia at Greve.
Enoteca on left . . . closed.

Peretola Airport outside Florence

the sequence because it has gone on for such a long time. I am curious if there is any pattern to the blasts. There is. It blows twelve seconds, is off forty five seconds, continues to blow two twelve second segments, and then be off fifteen seconds. That is a lot of noise in one's ears. This has been continuous for three hours.

Suddenly, a police car drives into the parking lot. It is Vigli Urbani, car number twenty three. A man and a woman, each in uniform, get out. The man leans against his door, watching the noisy car. The woman walks up to it. A family with a small son stops and looks at the back of the car as they pass. Two nuns walk by, shaking their heads. A man with a briefcase turns to look. The man and woman reenter Vigli Urbani, car number twenty three, drive around the square, observing, then, leave the parking lot entirely. The car's horn continues in the same order.

I keep a watch from my window. Ten minutes go by. Back comes Vigli Urbani, car number twenty three. It parks directly behind the car. Down the other side of the street appears a wrecker. All this time, guarding the French Consulate, which is on the other side of the parking lot and directly across the street from our hotel, is a large Italian polizia van, full of personnel. Obviously curious about what is happening behind them, and undoubtedly bored watching the door of a Consulate which has shown no action all afternoon, they get out to see. The door of the van is left wide open. If ever there might be an ideal time to assault that Consulate it is now. No one pays it the slightest attention. The opened-door polizia van is empty.

The driver of the wrecker sizes up the situation. With a nod of approval from the people of Vigli Urbani, car number twenty three, he opens the hood of the car. Three porters from our hotel walk over to watch. The horn is stifled. Tranquillity at last! Lovely quiet. What bliss, this total silence. The driver of the wrecker and the police visibly argue whether or not the car should be hauled away. The police do not want this done. They keep shaking their heads at the driver of the wrecker who does. They write a violation ticket and slip that under the car's windshield wiper.

The man from the wrecker slams his door and drives off in a huff. His services were not used. He could not collect a towing fee. He is disgruntled at being inconvenienced. The Italian guards get back into their van and resume watching the Consulate. Vigli Urbani, car number twenty three, drives off. The porters come back inside our hotel.

The car is quiet — no more tooting. All alone with no one paying the slightest attention, its parking lights are shining brightly.

$$\mathcal{C}$$

Italy: the triumph of form over substance!

While strolling beside the Arno River toward the United States Consulate, imagine our surprise when we spot a piece of sculpture similar to one we bought in Switzerland. It is sitting on the balcony of the top apartment of a four-storied building, an unusual bit of decoration on the normally austere buildings. It sparkles in the sunlight, a piece created by Gidon Graetz, fabricated in stainless steel. With all the Renaissance art in Florence, how unexpected something so totally modern. Someone here enjoys the type of modern art we do. We know the Graetz family lives in Fiesole and look forward to seeing them.

Walking along the sidewalks and streets of Florence can be difficult. The sidewalks follow the twisty, narrow streets which are paved in cobblestone. Some sidewalks are narrow, wide enough for one person. Another person coming from the opposite direction must step into the street when passing. One must pay heed to what one may step on too. No curb your dog laws here obviously!

⁊

There are many elderly Italians in this city, both men and women. They are interesting to watch. Some are quite handsome. Thinking of our parents and how it is more difficult for them to get around, we marvel that no one here trips, loses balance or falls on these uneven sidewalks. So many spots are toe stubbers if feet are not properly lifted. Must be difficult for toddlers too.

⁊

Walking down a long stone staircase in an old villa, I slip on the irregular worn tread of the last two steps just before the landing. I try to catch myself by grabbing for the rope banister on the wall, but it was too wiggly to steady the weight of my body. The heel of my left foot touching the eroded tread totally unbalances my body and causes my right foot to slip too.

Down I go with a loud thud as I fall onto the slippery stones. I slid around the landing and bounce on down two more stairs before coming to a stop. It is a smashing entrance into the living room!

🕮

While falling I feel the bones inside my left shoulder rise inside my body, and the wrist of my right arm scrape on the stone stairs. The thumb of my right hand is pulled back toward my wrist as I try desperately to stop this tumble. Luckily I neither hit my head nor back. When my body finally is still, the breath is knocked out of me for a minute or so. How lucky I am not to have been seriously hurt. Only my right lower arm sustained a huge black and blue mark from my silver cuff bracelet. Later on the thumb on that hand becomes quite swollen. My left shoulder grows sore and stiff too, but no broken bones from this incident at all, thank heaven.

🕮

Worn stair steps such as these are very real hazards. Rope banisters are picturesque but useless when really needed, but then everywhere in Italy are flimsy banisters or stone stairways with no railing support at all. Everybody should take heed. Safety codes prevent this type of construction in the United States.

🕮

I am in a store trying on a new pair of shoes, scarpe. I am having difficulty making them go on my feet.

The young salesgirl says to me, "Let me get a horn-shoe."

§

The Fenyes family have made a change in their lives. They bought a house in the country. This is a major commitment, financially, and even more so spiritually. Giovanna is a native Florentine, and she and Alberto have lived in the city since they were married. We are invited to see the new place and want to bring a housewarming present for the whole family. We know they have garden space. Being able to walk on grass and grow trees and flowers is a prime reason for their move.

§

Mac and I decide to buy an olive tree for their garden. Not having any idea where to acquire such a tree in Florence, or if it is possible, we ask our concierge. He can not believe we want to buy a tree. What will we do with an olive tree? Take it to the United States? No?! Finally, he concludes we really do want to buy this tree but for reasons he cannot quite comprehend. He suggests we go to the agricultural school. They have the best plant stock in Florence. We hail a taxi and give the driver the address.

With a lot of Mac's help, the driver finds the place. He does not have customers who buy trees and certainly not foreign ones so he is not familiar how to get there. It is easy to choose a beautiful little tree. With its roots embedded in a large ball of earth and securely bagged in plastic, we lug it back to the taxi. It is quite heavy. The driver helps load it onto the backseat. It is too tall to fit into the trunk. Mac, sitting in the front seat beside the driver, instructs him to return to the hotel.

Curiosity overcomes the driver. He asks if we are from the United States. Well, then, where in the United States? The tree will be planted there? The next fifteen minutes in a combination of English and Italian, Mac explains we are not taking the tree to the United States. He patiently tells the driver the climate where we live is too cold, troppo freddo, for olive trees to grow. We buy this tree for Italian friends. The driver does not comprehend. In fact, he is much concerned: How can we live where olive trees do not grow? How do we eat without olives and olive oil?

At this point, happily, we pull up in front of the hotel. What a relief! So many questions. I am giggling to myself in the back seat. The doorman greets us with a big smile.

"Oh, Signor Whiting, you buy an olive tree! Where are you going to plant it? In the United States? Oh, no, why not?"

So it went. Everyone has a lively interest in our purchase. There probably never was a foreigner who after purchasing a tree, stayed with it at the Excelsior Hotel. Made fascinating gossip all week long.

Everyday when Giovanna comes for Italian lessons, we hide the tree in the clothes closet so she will not see it. We savor this marvelous surprise for the Fenyes family.

193

Finally the weekend arrives. We take the tree down to the lobby in the elevator and load it into our rented car. We are off to the Fenyes home which is in a newly developed subdivision. They shout with joy when we appear at their front door with a four foot high, live olive tree. What a total surprise. Alberto says, "I can't believe you brought us a live tree, an olive tree at that!"

He immediately finds a shovel. We all turn over a scoop of sod in commemoration of the first olive tree to grow on the Fenyes' new property. He finishes the job properly as we stand around and supervise. There are tears in his eyes as he thanks both of us. Presenting them a living tree to grow in their own garden means so much, particularly to him. Of all the people we encounter Alberto is the most sentimental.

℅

We wander around the Fenyes new neighborhood, admiring handsome roses growing in many of the yards. Rosebushes seem to grow everywhere in this Florentine area. The soil and climate must be perfect for them. We see every kind and color rose from climbers to bushes to trees. We enjoy them hanging from walls along the road or in gardens. Their blossoms are enormous as are their thorns. When we were given some cut from a garden, they seemed to last forever.

℅

When the English discovered Italy was a pleasant place to live and started establishing homes, they brought with them their English concept of gardening. Their gardens had large vistas of grass and shade trees. There were beds of assorted varieties of annuals and perennials in as many colors as could be hybridized. They imposed this English know-how on the Italians.

It depends on one's point of view whether this is more desirable than the Italian unstructured gardens and natural colored flowers.

❦

Italians take flowers as they grow in nature without trying to hybridize them into colors unusual for the variety.

For example, iris is light lavender, pale yellow or soft white. One does not see any shades of mahogany. These flowers are planted along driveways, in terracotta pots, and, of course, in gardens. They grow in profusion. Terracotta pots are made in every size and shape. Every kind of flower, shrub, and, sometimes trees are planted in them. Everything seems to grow well. Anything looks handsome planted this way. We are inspired to try this type of gardening at our mountain home.

❦

Some of the prettiest potted flowering shrubs are the azaleas. They bloom in a multitude of white, magenta or pink blossoms. These plants live a long time. Some of them that we have seen in huge terracotta pots have thick, knotted stalks. This is obviously the result of many years growth. Some of these pots are reinforced with heavy wire rings knotted around them. This is an attempt to stop breakage of the pot from frost or bumping. We have also seen rhododendrons and lemon trees in enormous pots.

౯

The type of flowers Italians like best are the old fashioned varieties like pinks, marigolds, calendulas, daisies, and geraniums. There are larkspur, salvia, primrose, fuschia, snapdragons, pansies, zinnias and lavender too. Herbs are as much a part of the garden as flowers. Basil, rosemary and sage are very common. Any of these may be planted in pots or grow somewhat helter-skelter in a garden bed. All plants are cared for with love and infinite patience.

౯

Trees are pruned without mercy. They look butchered and stunted to our eye. The tops are taken out completely and the branches are chopped back severely. No small branch is allowed to grow. This makes a strange looking specimen. An old tree will be short with thick branches which have few leaves. Orchards are espaliered allowing the rows of trees to be closer together. These trees are generally cherry, peach, apple or pear. Olive trees are never espaliered, but they are pruned closely each spring.

᪐

Walking down a wide sidewalk one Sunday afternoon along with dozens of other strollers, Mac notices a young gypsy woman ahead. She is a pretty girl, flashily dressed in a red peasant blouse with a colorful printed skirt. Out of the corner of his eye he sees another older gypsy woman too. She is carrying a small baby wrapped in a shawl. To avoid walking into them, he moves to his left. The young woman moves to her right. The older woman, holding the baby, steps directly in front of him. This traps Mac against a railing at the edge of the sidewalk. Suddenly, he feels a hand in his trouser pocket. Instantly Mac reacts, aggressively lifting both his elbows up to his shoulder height. This knocks the old woman off stride. Mac pushes the younger woman aside and quickly walks ahead. The old gypsy shouts and raises her fist at him. The arrogant old woman is complaining loudly he might have hurt the baby!

᪐

Had Mac not reacted immediately and vigorously, he would have been robbed of everything in his pockets. Lucky for him was the clumsiness of the young gypsy pickpocket. Undoubtedly she was a beginner in the trade.

𝑔

After that experience we keep our eyes open for gypsies. We will cross any street to avoid encountering them another time. Are we subjecting gypsies to unfair discrimination?

𝑔

Shortly after this episode I happened to look out our hotel window one morning. There in the parking lot is another young gypsy with two young children. She is changing the diaper of the baby, placing the child on her shawl which is stretched out on the pavement of the parking lot. Finishing the task, she furtively looks around. Seeing no attendant, she picks up the baby and takes the other child by the hand. Drawing her shawl around the baby, she walks off, leaving a pile of plastic bags of rubbish where she had been.

𝑔

Many a little Italian girl around four or five years of age wears a pleated skirt which hang to her ankles. I reason to myself it must be that length so she can use it a long time. Looks a bit bizarre on such a small figure.

𝑔

And, there goes a police dog with his master taking a

stroll. The dog is sleek, proud, obviously intelligent. The master is pear-shaped, modest, a bit self-conscious. A wonderful study in contrasts. Who is taking whom for the walk?

Today Mac counted sixty-two cars driving along the Lungarno before he found one person using a seat belt.

Yesterday he stopped counting at a hundred. Not one person wore a seat belt!

We approach a policeman in Florence to ask street directions. We speak to him in Italian. A man, standing beside the policeman, turns and says in English to us, "Are you English?"

"Si," we both reply.

After a dinner at I Tre Pini restaurant at Pozzolatico we are driving back to Florence. We pass a runner, two runners and even more runners and realize we are in the midst of a marathon. What a strange time to be running, we think, as it is dark enough for us to use the car's headlights. Before we finish twisting down this road onto the wider city one, we pass sixty runners. Daytimes we dodge the bicyclists, nighttimes marathoners. What next?

☙

Bicycling seems to be the only sport seriously pursued by the Italians for exercise. Weekends the country roads are hazardous to drive dodging around them. They love to form a small group, dress in similar costumes, and careen up and down and around the bends and curves of the roads at furious speeds. How hot and tired some of those men look!

☙

A literal translation from La Nazione, a national Italian newspaper, by Mac:

"A delicate type mentally and physically, then, this crazy Mike, who at the age of six lost his mother in an automobile accident, was raised by his sisters, Palmira and Maria, (the latter known as 'the Old Maid'), in his youth a jack of all trades, migrated to Germany, where he worked as an operator at Volkswagen, returned to Naples, joined the smuggling ring of cigarettes and blue hulls, rose up the ladder to become 'numero uno' of his family. He is a millionaire. Those who know him well say that every now and then Mr. Zaza asserts that he is the Count of Montecristo, in the sense that his wealth serves only to help avenge his enemies. At all times, remember those in his circle, in the house of the boss

200

everything feminine must not be profaned: the bitch and the tabby must be called 'ladies,' and when he has visitors his wife, Anna Maria Liguori, (graduate in languages of the Sorbonne, with dual citizenship, Italian and French, thanks to her mother who came from Grenoble), must pack up and go to the home of Maria, the Old Maid. For Mr. Zaza his wife is to be revered like the madonna. When she ended up in jail, he flew into such a rage that he said to Judge Francesco Nitto Palma—who had ordered the arrest of the couple and others of the clan—'If you don't release my wife immediately, I will have yours killed, and if you aren't married, I will have your mother killed.' The judge was not intimidated and the boss cooled down."

I am walking alone down the Lungarno when I hear a siren. Is it a police car or an ambulance? Sirens are heard all the time so I pay little attention to this one and continued walking. The sound gets so loud I glance over my shoulder to see what is happening.

It is a police car, coming in my direction. It is being driven fast. With its siren screaming, lights on top flashing, never slowing for the considerable traffic, it is forcing its way through all the vehicles, bulldozing down the street. Cars swerve side to side opening a path. The police car persists relentlessly. If an automobile does not move, the police bump into it as a signal to turn aside. This causes panic among the drivers. Cars do shift. Some run up onto sidewalks. Others collide into each other. There is a general dinning racket of steel hitting steel, brakes screeching, and drivers starting and stopping in jerky spurts. The police are absolutely brutal. They continue with never a pause, paying no heed to the confusion. People, like me, who are walking along the sidewalk, stop to watch. I jump into the first doorway nearest me and stand there spellbound. Such chaos and for what?

Soon the police car disappears from sight, and the untangling begins. Little by little everything gets back to normal. If one can ignore a few dented fenders and scratched bumpers, it would seem nothing out of the ordinary has happened. I wonder if all that ruthlessness did not cause more damage than good. I never learn the rationale for this exercise of authority.

☙

Along a side street in Florence we see smoke coming from a window of one of the apartment buildings. We judge it to be from the third or fourth floor. There is no one else on the street, and we wonder whether we should alert someone. Suddenly a clang clanging announces the arrival of a fire truck. The street is so narrow, and the truck is so wide it is inching its way along. A few heads pop out from windows opposite the smoking one. The fire truck is almost there. More heads materialize. The truck stops, and rubber-booted firemen get out. They are dressed head to toe in heavy, yellow waterproof suits. They lug the hose from the back of the truck. Looking up they see it will not reach the smoking window so they drop it onto the pavement. Heads shake seeing this. The firemen unfasten the ladder from the side of the truck and prop it against the wall of the building. It is too short to reach the smoking window. We all look up, wondering what they will do, but there is no smoke— absolutely none whatsoever! Someone yells something. Heads nod and disappear inside. The firemen replace their hose and ladder. They get into the fire truck and begin backing it out of the street. What in the world? we wonder. We learn an overheated frying pan caused the smoke. Nothing dramatic like an apartment on fire. Just another incident in a busy day.

Molto fumo e poco arrosto! Much smoke and little fire or lots of noise and not much action, a characteristic of quite a few Italians.

"Signori! Come va? How nice to see you. Come in, come in!"

This greeting Mac and I often hear when we walk into a restaurant. Perhaps it is some time since we have dined there. The greeting is always the same. What a pleasure being remembered and having people genuinely as happy to see us as we are to see them.

§

We prefer small restaurants, ones with ten tables or less.

205

They are easy to spot as their front window always exhibits whatever is fresh and available to enjoy that day. Occasionally it might be a bottle of a special wine. We have seen displays of bunches of beautiful fresh asparagus, large clusters of zucchini with their yellow flowers left on the stem, and once an impressive basket of huge porcini mushrooms. Whatever it is, your mouth waters in anticipation. Inside you walk by food trolleys. One may be filled with a variety of freshly picked greens for salad. Another has the dolci, Italian sweets, cake creations topped with white powdered sugar. Perhaps, also, there is a bowl of profiteroles, those luscious little pastry puffs filled with soft cream and topped with bitter chocolate sauce. Undoubtedly there is a bowl of tiramisu. (Literally translated this means, "pick-me-up"!) That delicious concoction is made of sweet, soft mascarpone cheese, egg yolks, sugar, Marsala wine, and cream combined and cooked into a soft custard, which is then poured over layers of espresso coffee flavored ladyfingers. The dessert is finished with a heavy sprinkling of bitter chocolate powder.

Italian meals are generally two courses followed by a dolce and coffee. You decide how you wish those courses to be. The first is called piatto primo, the first plate or course. This can be a choice of a vegetable or a pasta or a soup. The piatto secondo, the second plate or course, follows and might be meat or fish, but it could also be simply a vegetable, or a salad or a pasta. It is your decision to eat as food appeals to your appetite that day. Vegetables are not served on the same plate with a fish or meat. Salad is a definite course, not an accompaniment. Antipasto, hors d'oeuvres, start the meal only if desired.

€

We appreciate the interest shown by the waiters in helping you choose what you wish to eat rather than having them encourage you to eat some dish they want to sell. They care and want very much for you to have a memorable meal at their table. Restaurants take great pride in preparing your meal. No reheated pasta here! Every dish is cooked when it is ordered, never before. Often you eat the first course before you order the second. And, you still have no long wait.

€

It is interesting how the young sons and nephews are brought into the business by their fathers and uncles as waiter helpers. There is so much pride in the service of food in this country. Eating is a serious and much appreciated business.

€

We thoroughly enjoy the simplicity of Italian food. No sauces mask what is underneath. Powdered garlic is never used as seasoning. Americans have the mistaken idea Italians use quantities of garlic. In northern Italy fresh garlic, not powdered garlic, is used with mild, subtly flavored foods, like fish, to perk it up. It is never combined with strongly flavored foods. Sometimes in the United States at the same meal Americans will be served pasta flavored with garlic and garlic buttered bread, followed by meat cooked with garlic, then a green salad with a strong garlic dressing and think they are eating a good Italian food. Italians consider this most unappetizing. It truly offends their sensibilities as it does ours.

A waiter with a great sense of humor is serving a woman customer. He is loudly singing the tenor's aria from an Italian opera while soulfully looking into her eyes and simultaneously placing the food on her plate.

Observing us watching him, he comes over to our table and asks us if we have noticed the table with the Japanese diners.

"Yes," we say.

He asks if we know why Japanese eyes are squinted.

"No," we say, "why are Japanese eyes squinted?"

"Because," he answers, mimicking a Japanese in making his own eyes slant and pretending to talk with their accent by not being able to pronounce the sound R, "they are always saying, 'my God, more lice!'" And off he walks, howling with laughter at his cleverness.

I would not be surprised to see a sign in any restaurant saying, "kiss the cook." Old customers are apt to do just that before they sit down to enjoy their meal.

ε

We walk into the restaurant promptly on time for our reservation. Since it is a small place, it is easy to note how all the tables are positioned as we wait to be seated. Tonight there is one long table for fourteen people and another for eight which take up most of the room. All other tables are against the walls and are set for two or four people. "Ah ha, a really big party," we think.

We wait an extra long time to be seated. We note two waiters break a table away from the long fourteen-people table. They move it aside and motion us to it. We are amused and realize they probably have misplaced our hotel's request for a reservation. We pretend not to notice anything amiss, and they make believe this was the table reserved just for us.

We order and start eating our dinner.

Suddenly, in come four or five beautifully dressed females with escorts. All the women have on red silk dresses, the bright red associated with Christmas, and a lot of glittery jewelry. One seldom sees jewelry in restaurants, and never four or five women in the same party wearing identically colored costumes. Whatever the difference in style each dress is totally lost in this sea of red. They might as well be four or five clones as their personal individuality is totally lost. They arrange themselves at the table set for eight people.

We continue eating.

A large group of men come in. Everyone in the restaurant looks up at this noisy intrusion. They head for the long table seating fourteen, only now it is set for twelve people. Twelve men sit down. Four or five men are left standing. With much ado the waiters push a few extra chairs around the table, and a chair is placed at either end. This crowds our table. We quietly bodily pick it up and move it further away from the big one and continue eating. Everybody is seated and apparently not too squeezed together. Rearranging the seating is just an ordinary occurrence at a restaurant, even if other guests are in the middle of their meal.

℅

People generally dislike having to tell anyone no. Italians can hardly tolerate doing it. "No, we have no table left this evening," or "No, we did not make porridge for breakfast this morning," are simple examples. When we stayed at the Certosa di Maggiano as we checked in we made our dinner reservation. Even if you are a guest of a hotel, it is always best to book a reservation for dinner to be assured a seat in the dining room. This can be especially important at smaller hotels.

℅

We note the girl tells us how busy they are when we ask for early seating in our hotel dining room. She does not say they cannot take us, but she does not confirm our table

210

reservation when she writes our name on the first seating list. Five minutes before we are to be in the dining room, a knock at the door of our suite. The girl from the front desk is there, full of smiles but wringing her hands. She is so sorry. They have overbooked the restaurant. They will be happy to seat us an hour hence. Will this be convenient? "But of course!" we answer. If we want to eat, that will have to be convenient. Had she told us they were overbooked when we checked in, we might have had the option of choosing to go elsewhere, even perhaps dressing for dinner later. It is so hard to say no and possibly disappoint a guest.

A favorite of ours for a quick lunch is a panino. This is a sandwich made from a roll with a crusty outside and chewy inside. The roll, intentionally unbuttered, is cut lengthwise and stuffed with meat or cheese, occasionally fresh vegetables. Neither butter nor sauce seems necessary.

We like them with prosciutto. Each day panini are freshly made and can be bought at coffee bars in any town or at comfort stations along the autostrada. This simply prepared food tastes so good.

Looking for the turn to Radda we pass a little town called La Villa. There is a small restaurant beside the road that appears nice so we decide to lunch there before continuing.

We park the car and walk inside through a curtain of dangling strings of colored beads. There is a seedy deli on the left with wonderful looking sausages hanging from the ceiling and round loaves of dark, crusty bread in the glass case and on the small wooden counter. Straight ahead is another room, looking much like a living room. Since there is no signora to tell us where to go, we simply walk into that room. It definitely belongs to the family with its upholstered sofa and chairs. Turning right is a huge adjoining kitchen. We see the dining room is to the left and quickly head in that direction.

ε

A waitress waves us to table number four. We sit down at a rustic table for six people, set with a red checkered cloth, a fork, knife and napkin at each place. It is unpretentious, but clean. The waitress comes and suggests we try the ravioli. It is fresh that morning. We ask also if they have prosciutto and melon, and they do. She brings us a bottle of water, white wine in a crockery pitcher, and slices of the crusty bread. We look around as we break off some to chew.

There are five other tables of people in this room. Table one has a single man who eats bread covered with fresh garlic slices. Before each bite he dips it into olive oil in a soup bowl in front of him. He munches reading his newspaper. Table two has a German man and woman. She stares at me and continues to do so the entire meal. Table three seats two truck drivers, each with his newspaper and turned a complete ninety degrees away from each other. They never say a word the entire meal. Table four is us. Table five seats a young man and his girlfriend. She is impressed with his lengthy ordering of their meal in Italian. Afterwards they speak entirely in English. Table six has a plain looking man and woman who eat pasta and occasionally speak quietly to each other. It is a strange ambiance, this dining room. It is so quiet I can hear the chomping of the crunchy bread at tables one and two.

⌇

Our waitress is a heavyset, bosomy woman with dyed, black hair. She has on a shapeless cotton dress with a small apron tied at her waist. She shuffles in and out. Going up to table three, she says, "Pasta, signori?" "Si," they answer. Then, "No, you cannot have meat sauce on the ravioli!" The German couple and ourselves laugh quietly at her brusque behavior.

⌇

Our meal is delicious. The bread is excellent. The melon is ripe and juicy and blends so well with the dried, salty, home-cured ham. The ravioli is served with a slaver of butter on top and sprinkled with freshly ground black pepper. We eat and enjoy. Once again the best restaurants prove to be the little unprepossessing places operated mostly for the villagers. This one is run by two women with their daughters and someone else's grandmother.

❧

Fiori fritti, zucchini squash flowers lightly coated with beaten egg, dusted with flour, then deep-fried, are as tasty a vegetable to eat as can be imagined. They are fried crisp. When served, the flower is definitely visible and still yellow in color. A good cooking trick! Italians know how to cook vegetables so tasty, they are often chosen as a course in a meal. One desires nothing else with them other than, perhaps, a slice of Tuscan bread and a glass of wine.

❧

Interestingly, bottled water is always served with every meal. After one sits at the table, the first question the waiter will ask is what one wants to drink, vino, wine, and acqua, water, with gas, con gas, or without gas, acqua minerale naturale. He is not insulted whether both water and wine or only one is ordered. Generally everybody has a bottle of water on the table, which is empty when the diners leave the table.

❧

These water bottles are interesting to study. They all have labels with the analysis of the water's components like the percentage of calcium, sodium, magnesium, or bicarbonate. Also along the side of the label are punched holes showing the month and day when this particular bottle was filled.

It goes without saying it is always safest for one's health to drink bottled water.

꿈

"Yes, we have piselli. How would you like them served—with burro, panna, olio di oliva or formaggio?" With butter, cream, olive oil or cheese? Are you ever offered such a choice as this in restaurants in the United States, not to mention expecting green peas picked fresh from the garden that morning?

꿈

Corn is never served as a separate vegetable and is unthinkable eaten from the cob. This vegetable is grown only for animal consumption. It is ground into meal for human use. This custom is widespread throughout Europe.

꿈

Minestrone soup is best with the addition of a little olive oil, po' d'olio. Relieves the sharp taste of the soup.

꿈

There is a short span of time when freshly picked porcini are in season. These are enormous specimens of the mushroom family. Some might be as much as eight or ten inches across or even wider. The Italians cook them in a variety of ways, often grilled like steak. Every restaurant announces they are in season by placing a basketful in their front window. They are offered daily until the season passes.

☙

One particular noon I am eating deliciously broiled porcini with Giovanna and Alberto Fenyes when Mac, sitting across from me, suddenly fades from my vision. I blink, sip my San Pellegrino water, and take another bite of porcini. I presume I am imagining things. I look, and again he blurs as I stare at him. My legs feel numb too.

Giovanna, Alberto and Mac are deep in conversation and not noticing I am unusually quiet. Hoping to quickly feel better I drink a larger amount of water. My skin feels prickly and hot. Giovanna turns to me and asks if I am not going to finish my porcini, may she? They taste so good to her. My leg muscles are shaky. I feel nauseous and extremely sick to my stomach. I must leave and quickly.

I signal Mac by standing up. I can hardly move! What is happening? Mac sees I am in trouble and gets up from his chair to help. My legs are so numb. They do not feel a part of my body! I can barely walk to the door of the restaurant and do so only with Mac's help. The Fenyes stay seated, realizing I am ill, but do not need their help. Mac leads me outside. I gulp fresh air into my lungs as deeply as I can. This clears my head a bit. Mac insists I lean against the building to rest. Passers-by stare. I am embarrassed to make such a spectacle of myself. The nausea subsides, but the weakness does not.

Mac and I then realize I must be having a severe toxic reaction from the porcini. It has poisoned me. There was no doubt it is the porcini since I have eaten nothing else. With greatest difficulty I slowly am able to walk back to the hotel —a mere two blocks from the restaurant. Mac puts his arm across my shoulders and almost carries me. I still do not have good control of my legs. Each step I am not sure I can go further because I have so little feeling in them.

Once in our room I collapse onto the bed, grateful to be there. A good sleep made me better, but it was a day or so before the weakness left. Never a bite of porcini has touched my lips henceforth. That was a very scary experience.

℃

The Italians simply cannot bake potatoes correctly. Since they are not a common part of the Italian diet, this is not surprising. Giovanna is most puzzled because she thinks the process is so complicated. We have several conversations about this, always ending with Giovanna's comment: "But, you don't eat the skin, do you, Mr. Whiting?" visibly shuddering at the mere thought.

℃

So one day I wrote this note to her:

217

To Giovanna—

It's just a potato you are baking so first of all—relax! It is going to do all the work! (Alberto, reading over Giovanna's shoulder laughs and says, "That's it, Giovanna. Relax! That is the right attitude when you cook!")

Here is exactly what to do:

1. Turn on the stove's oven. We figure it should be set at 200°C or the dial set a little hotter than medium heat.
2. Plan one potato for each person served.
3. Wash each potato under running water and dry each potato.
4. Put potatoes on oven rack, keeping them apart from each other. (Your oven rack should be in the center of the oven.)
5. The potatoes probably will need to bake 1-hour 15 minutes or 1-hour 20 minutes. Set your timer to know when this is or have somebody at home watch the time for you.
6. It is a good idea half way through the baking to do this: prick the skin of each potato with a fork. This releases the steam and helps "dry out" the inside so the potato will be flaky and dry when served. Continue cooking.
7. When potatoes are done, you tell this by pricking them with a fork. If the fork goes easily into the potato, and the skin on the outside is crispy, the potato is ready to be served. Do not take them out of the oven until you are ready to eat them.

8. To serve: Cut down the middle (the long side of the potato) with a sharp knife. Use something to keep your hands from burning, take hold of the potato on either end and push the ends toward the center. Do this just enough to get the white of the potato broken up a bit. Put cold butter on the white part as well as salt and pepper. Serve one to each person.
9. Do eat the skins. They are good with more butter and salt and pepper. They are best when eaten crispy and crunchy.

Q.B.

ℰ

This is written in great detail. Hopefully everything is explained step by step. Now I want to give you a shorter version:

Set the oven to 200ºC. Wash/dry potatoes. Bake 1-hour 15 to 1-hour 20 minutes. Prick with fork halfway through baking. Potato is done when soft in center and crisp outside. Serve hot with butter, salt and pepper.
Potatoes cannot be overcooked.

Q.B.

ℰ

Q.B. These initials mean quanto basta. Translated this

means as much as is enough! It is found in many old Italian cookbooks at the conclusion of a recipe. I asked Giovanna why. She says she does not know exactly what it does mean. Perhaps it refers to the amount of ingredients used or the time to cook something, she guesses, but she is not a cook, and those initials are just there!

ℰ

In return for the potato recipe Giovanna and Alberto both want me to have their recipe for making tomato sauce. This is what they tell me to do:

Use very ripe tomatoes, the Roma type. Wash and place in a kettle. Add salt, pepper and a lot of basil.

"Well, how much?" I ask.

"Oh, you know, a lot!" they reply. They, of course, mean fresh basil.

They add a carrot and celery. If the taste of an onion is desired, add that too. In addition Giovanna says she adds a piece of hot, red pepper. All these ingredients simmer together at least two hours. The mixture is then pureed and stored until ready to use. They add a bit of olive oil to the top of the bottle before corking it. This helps keep the sauce from fermenting. When using the sauce, they add a bit of olive oil to it. They emphasize the importance of using ripe tomatoes.

ℰ

Dining one evening at Omero, a favorite trattoria, the unexpected takes place. A threesome is seated at the table beside us. The fourth in their party turns out to be a Pekingese dog! Since this breed is a great favorite of mine, I initiate a conversation with the woman nearest to me. She smiles and nods, but it is the man in the group who asks me about my Peke, Tarka. The Peke who is the cause of all this conversation gives me the typical bored look only a Pekingese can command, blinks, and promptly falls asleep in the chair.

The antipasto is brought. The Peke shows no interest, but as soon as the next course is served, the Peke sits up and barks. This causes a terrible commotion. All three people tell her to hush. The woman beside me feeds her a piece of the lovely steak Florentine, cooked to perfection—dark on the outside, but soft and rare inside, salted and served with a little lemon. The Peke chews with contentment and is perfectly quiet until she wants another piece. This dog, no dumbbell, knows what is good. I am amused.

We watch throughout our dinner. The people consume three full bottles of red wine and turn out to be Spaniards, not Italians. I realize they did not understand any of our conversation about Tarka, not comprehending my English at all.

Mac and I are ordering our usual meal for luncheon— insalata verde, formaggio, pane di campagna, e vino bianco. Mac asks for an order of salsiccia too. Sitting next to us are a man and a woman, young-looking, sightseers, we presume, observing a large Canon camera sitting on their table. They are conversing quietly. They are casually dressed—he in slacks and an open-neck t-shirt, she in a light colored cotton dress. Both are extremely obese. Fat people like this are not often seen here.

We begin eating and happen to notice the food trolley being rolled up to the couple's table. On it is a huge steak, vegetables and a large serving of french fried potatoes. A waiter carefully proportions the food between the two. Since it is more of a dinner menu than a luncheon one, we watch intrigued as they consume everything on their plates, obviously enjoying each bite. The dessert trolley is wheeled over to them. We have ordered espresso with biscotini, a variety of small cookies. Curiosity makes us watch what this couple shall choose for dessert. Perhaps they will refuse. What a good idea after such a heavy meal! No, he chooses lemon pie, indicating a large wedge. She is served a large piece of fruit tart. This is lunch! What, we wonder, will be their dinner choices only a few hours hence? Ten years from now will these two be alive? We dare not speculate. When any Italian eats heavily at noon, they eat lightly that evening. Let us pray these young Americans do the same tonight. They are in danger of ruining their health from seriously overeating.

⁂

People here talk about going to the bar or meeting you at a bar. They are going to a coffee bar to have a cup of espresso and inviting you to have one with them. Other times they might have a glass of freshly squeezed orange juice and a sugary little pastry too. Alcoholic drinks are available too.

☙

"Have you ever been to a fett'unta?" asks our friend Gerardo Kraft.

"A what?"

"A fett'unta. You must come to ours," he says, totally ignoring our question. "We have friends visiting from Switzerland who come each year for it. You must too. It is tomorrow."

"But, what is a fett'unta, Gerardo?" We still wonder what he is inviting us to do.

"Just come tomorrow at noon. You'll see. Oh, don't wear your best clothes. Here's the address. We'll expect you at the frantoia, the factory!" Gerardo is off.

☙

Next day we arrive at what looks like a small warehouse. We decide it is the correct place as we recognize Gerardo's large Fiat parked beside the building. We walk around and find a side door open. We hesitantly stick our heads inside. A wood fire burns on an open hearth. The rather dark room has a rough stone floor, cement block walls and a couple of windows bringing in some light. It must be the frantoia we decide. Two very large-boned women are walking around. Upon second look we see they are nuns! They walk through the room, carrying huge baskets over their arms. Each is dressed in black habit, head covered, sleeves rolled up to elbow, and skirt to the ankles. They wear high laced, heavy soled, black leather shoes. Their dresses are protected with long white aprons, crucifixes dangling back and forth across their chests. What a strange atmosphere! Then, we see the Krafts.

℞

"Hello, here we are! You found us without trouble?" greets Karin. "Please, come over."

She has a table set up in one corner of the room with eight chairs around it. It is covered with a linen tablecloth and beautifully set with dishes and silverware, ready for luncheon, a soup bowl in front of each place. On the table are various serving dishes of foods to pass and glasses for wine. At one end Gerardo is cutting a loaf of Italian bread and putting slices, fette, on a metal grill apparently to be toasted in the fireplace.

℞

The nuns walk past us, with baskets full of olives. Some have twigs still dangling on their stems from harvesting. Gerardo explains they have picked the olives themselves and are taking them over to the mull in the other room. After the olives (including the twigs, which make for a better flavor oil, we are told) are mashed, the paste is piped to the other side of the room. There it is extruded onto circular, cocoa colored brush mats, which are held in place by a metal rod down the center. When the mat is fully covered with olive paste, another is lowered onto it until about a dozen or eighteen mats are so accumulated on the central pipe. Downward pressure is then applied from above. The oil squeezed from this process is designated extra virgine. It is a bright, clear dark green and smells delicious. The second and third pressings are not considered quite as elegant and are used for cooking.

We all are witnessing the making of this year's crop of olive oil and will sample the new batch. This is what a fett'unta luncheon is to celebrate.

❦

The factory is one of the few small primitive ones left in Italy. We of course realize with the quantity of olive oil used in Italy each year it must be manufactured in huge factories. It is a poignant experience to watch these independent, cheerful nuns going about manufacturing their own, doing the entire process themselves. We admire their strength and individuality. It is no easy job.

❦

Gerardo toasts the bread slices over the fire. We each are given a slice to put in our soup bowl. We are instructed to rub a piece of newly peeled fresh garlic on it. A pitcher of the just pressed olive oil is passed. We are to pour a small or large amount, each individual chooses how much, of the oil onto our warm toast. We sprinkle a bit of salt too. Now we may eat fett'unta. (Roughly translated it means an "oiled slice", which it certainly is.)

Everybody at the table plunges their forks into the mixture except Mac and I. We are a bit skeptical how our stomachs will react to such a concentrated dose of olive oil. Of course, when we try, we find it delicious, but extremely rich. Others enjoy seconds and some thirds. Not us! One slice is all we dare. It is very filling.

Gerardo then asks how we like our steak grilled. The feast continues, and the afternoon passes on. During one lull in the pressing the owner comes by. We invite him to drink a toast to the new olive oil. Stray dogs and cats chase each other in and out of the room and under and around our table. The nuns continue bringing in olives. The press squeezes more oil. The fire burns brightly. Its all very informal and friendly. A productive afternoon. One to remember long afterwards.

We are driving in a Fiat Strada (no more Ritmos for us!) to Prato on our way to an art gallery. We are to see an exhibition of mosaic pictures, an avant garde collection created with fragments of mirror, colored glass, marbles and bits of metals. These originals have been designed and executed by the wife of the president of Tuscany, whom we recently met. We are not keen on driving to Prato in the evening, but she is such an enthusiastic, ebullient person, it is impossible to refuse her invitation. Our friend, Gerardo, promises to guide us to the gallery.

&

We weave in and out of the evening traffic following his car. With us is a close friend from the United States. Against his better judgment, and only because I insist, he is sitting in front beside Mac, his seat belt tightly fastened. I tell him he may miss something interesting if he is in the rear. To be truthful I am happy to be in back. I can duck behind the front seats if I get jittery on this drive.

&

We converse back and forth, having a great time. Seems to me Mac is driving more speedily than usual. I wonder why, but do not mention it aloud. Gerardo, ahead of us, is moving extremely fast. He does not let a single car stay in front of him. As he goes by car after car, Mac keeps up passing the same automobiles. The moment Mac reaches Gerardo, Gerardo pulls farther ahead. It becomes a race to keep up with him.

&

I realize our American friend is extremely quiet. As a matter of fact he has said nothing for the past several minutes. One might say he is hunched down in his seat. I no longer can see the top of his head.

"Ethan," I ask, making casual conversation, "what are

you going to have for breakfast tomorrow?"

"Breakfast? Tomorrow?" he replies. "Helen, if I survive this ride, the traffic, such speed, Helen, I may not live that long!" We all laugh, but I know exactly how he feels.

℅

Later we ask Gerardo why he drove so rapidly.

"Oh, I thought every time you caught up to me that meant you wanted to go faster!" he replies with a big smile.

℅

We own an interesting mosaic of a golden sun god from that night's collection. Indeed, it was an entertaining show. Our hostess is a vision every bit as exciting as the exhibition we ultimately viewed. She is costumed in brown tight leather pants with thigh-high suede boots on her legs. A frothy chiffon, chestnut-colored, diaphanous blouse tops the trousers, revealing a generously endowed bosom. She effervescently greets a crowd of guests. The passed hors d'oeuvres are delicious and plentiful. The champagne is cold and bubbly. We never look at our sun god and recall this. We only remember that wild drive following Gerardo to Prato.

℅

"Where's Gary? Isn't he with you?"

229

"No, he's with you!" "But, he isn't. He drove you back from the auction."

"No, he didn't. We three and Plume drove back together, and he wasn't in our car."

℃

We have arrived at the entrance of the Park Palace Hotel and are talking with Giulio, Rosina, and Dorice who are walking the dachshund, Plume, in the garden beside the entrance. They beat us back from the auction. We assumed Gary would ride with them.

We had just attended an auction at the Villa delle Rose, a beautiful estate whose owners, The Diva, la signora, a renowned opera singer, and her husband, are selling. They are retiring to Switzerland. This auction is the social event of the season in Florence as the villa is also historically important. Many valuable antiques are slated to go on the block. The famous auction house of Sotheby is in charge. They had created and circulated a beautiful booklet describing the antiques to be offered. It is widely rumored the head of London Sotheby's, a Mr. Peter Wilson, and personal friend of The Diva's, will attend causing additional excitement. Perhaps he will conduct some of the auctioneering. This is news as he is of retirement age and seldom wields the gavel. Everybody who is anybody clamored for a ticket whether they wished to bid or not.

"We" are a group consisting of the Tamassys, Giulio and Rosina and their dachshund, Plume, who with their sister-in-law, Dorice, had driven here from Rome. Bill Davenport

230

came from Paris. Mac and I and Gary Stauffer all flew in from the United States. We invited Rosina, who is an art history teacher, to bid for us. We cannot understand Italian quickly enough to do it ourselves. Giulio de Tamassy, Rosina's husband is a sculptor and a movie set designer. He and Dorice came for the fun, and the family dog, Plume, always goes everywhere with them. He sat on Rosina's lap during the auction. Everytime the audience applauded when a particular outstanding piece was sold, Plume barked. After the first couple of times, everybody sitting close by laughed at his enthusiasm.

☙

The Villa delle Rose dates back to the fifteenth century. Originally built by the wine-producing Antinori family and it stayed in their possession until World War Two when it served as headquarters for the Germans. At another time during the war it also was used as a hospital. When The Diva and her husband bought it after the war, it was smoky, sooty, and in serious need of repair. They did a fantastic job of restoring. The frescoes, which the original family started, then added one room each century, were renovated and are especially nice.

☙

But, where is Gary? We realize he must be back at the villa. In the commotion of leaving Plume chased another dog

231

in the parking lot terrifying us he would be killed in the moving traffic. When we finally corral him into Tamassy's car, we are most happy to jump into ours and start driving back to the hotel. There is much maneuvering through very heavy traffic to get there. With so much confusion we apparently had left Gary behind. Tamassys assumed he was with us. Since he had driven them to the auction in Tamassy's car, we naturally assumed he was in their car on the return trip. Mac and I quickly turn around and hurry back for him.

⟨ε⟩

Meantime back at Villa delle Rose Gary looked around for us and realized we had gone without him. What to do? Obviously find a telephone and call for a taxi.

⟨ε⟩

By now the villa is almost deserted. There are only a few persons cleaning up after the auction. He goes up to one and asks to use the telephone. The man does not understand what Gary says. Gary gestures what he wants and is directed toward the telephone.

He dials his hotel.

"Hello? This is Dr. Stauffer. I would like you to send a taxi . . ."

"No, no!" says the person at the hotel. "Don't come. Don't come! We are full!"

"But, I need a taxi! This is Dr. Stauffer at the Villa delle Rose."

232

"No! No!!" says the person. "I said we are full, all full, no rooms, no rooms."

"But, this is Dr. Stauffer," Gary continues, "and I do have a room."

"No, no, Dr. Stauffer is upstairs in his room asleep."

"No, he isn't. I'm Dr. Stauffer."

"No, no, don't come, don't come, we are full." Bang, the man slams down the receiver.

Gary is stranded at Villa delle Rose!

𝓰

Mac and I finally make it back. Traffic is still heavy from the auction. There he is nonchalantly leaning on the villa's huge iron gate, looking very Noel Cowardish, casually smoking a cigarette! A guard is standing nearby impatient to lock the gate. How relieved we are to see each other. Then we start laughing at the nonsense of this entire evening. So many happenings. We laugh until tears come to our eyes. What an extraordinary event for us all.

𝓰

Gidon Graetz is a young Israeli who began his adult life by apprenticing in his father's shipping business. He worked out of Holland. He was to transfer to Livorno from there. On his way to Livorno he stopped in Florence. He was captivated by the restoration movement taking place after the flooding of the Arno river in the sixties, and the opportunity for him to learn sculpturing. He took a leave of absence from the family shipping business to study sculpturing, and he never went back to shipping again.

Gidon's father came to Florence and wanted to stay. The only way he could get a suitable place to live was to rent a castle with no option to buy. When he finally did get the opportunity to buy, he asked his family if he should. They all said, "No!" but he overruled them and bought Castel di Vinciliata after he sold his shipping business to the government of Israel.

℥

We telephone the Graetzs and ask if we might meet with them. We were first introduced by Brigitte de Almeida Lopes who owns Galerie Lopes in Zurich, Switzerland. She had a Graetz exhibition which we attended and bought one of his handsome stainless steel pieces. The Graetzs promptly invite us to tea at the castello. We are delighted to accept.

℥

On the appointed day we drive our car to Fiesole, then follow the directions Gidon gave us. We see Castel di Vinciliata long before we reach it. It is perched atop a high hill and overlooks all of Florence. Built from stone fragments of the original walls of Florence, it is a marvelous looking structure with a tower and crenelated roof line. Castelli originally were fortifications, and this one is no exception. It is totally surrounded by a stone wall. When arriving at the property, the car is parked outside its walls.

ᘐ

Gidon greets us as well as Sunniva, his beautiful Norwegian wife. She, togged out in corduroy pants and high leather boots, is finishing working in the vegetable garden so excuses herself to change. Gidon opens a low, wooden door in the stone wall and invites us into the grounds of the castello.

We all stoop to go through this door and step onto a pathway made of small pebbles and into a garden of tall, tall pine trees. An exciting sight greets us: At the end of this long path with a backdrop of an ancient stone wall and framed by garden greenery sits the original of our own Graetz sculpture. Its stainless steel is aglow in the late afternoon sunlight. What a welcome to us! Its radiance in this peaceful woody scene takes our breath away. The Graetz dogs run up to sniff us, then dash on down the path. We note more of Gidon's pieces strategically placed throughout the garden. Their stainless steel is luminous in this light. There are huge pots of blooming azaleas here and there, adding to the ambiance. Those plants must have lived in their containers a long time, judging by their size. It is a dramatic and quite beautiful approach to the castello.

ᘐ

235

The castello is on our left and does not seem as monumental as it appears from below on the road. It has a tower on one side, which seems to rise up forever. I immediately imagine playing "storm the castle" and ask Gidon if he ever did that when he was a boy. He said he did. We discuss whether it is more fun to be an attacker outside the tower, trying to get to the top, or be a defender on top keeping the attackers down. We agree either side has its special merits. It is fun to pretend such a siege.

The castle proper is on the other side of a wall with a gate, which is open. We can see into a courtyard which houses many more huge terracotta pots mostly of azaleas but some with lemon trees. We note a living room on the right, but are not invited to go in. We continue straight ahead, walking down a concrete sloped ramp into a formal garden. (In my imagination this ramp was used to haul the cannon!) The garden below it is full of snapdragons and marigolds, very appropriate for pretty bouquets. We turn left toward the terrace. Another Graetz piece sits on the low wall. Its flat, winged surface reflects Florence in the hazy horizon. Its silvery colored metal is turning a pinkish color as the sun begins dipping toward sunset.

$$\mathcal{E}$$

In this setting Sunniva is waiting. We are invited to a round wooden table with the suggestion we choose those seats which can best let our eyes feast on the panorama of the distant Florence and the spectacle of the deepening evening sunset. A uniformed maid brings out a tea tray. It is the most exquisite scene imaginable.

Suddenly, the air crackles with energy as a white-haired, stylishly coifed lady, a voluminous wool cape flying behind her, dashes in. She is dressed entirely in black with loads of silver jewelry—around her neck, on her ears, her fingers and her arms. With the poise of great self-confidence she positions herself firmly in a chair, at the same time saying, "How do you do, Mr. and Mrs. Whiting. How are you? Yes, Sunniva, I would like a cup of tea and a piece of cake." Gidon stands and says, "Mac and Helen, this is my Mother!" We greet her. She immediately insists we are not eating enough. Perhaps the cake. Her cook made it that morning, and it is very good. We must try some. She is fabulous! She dominates the conversation. We hear the history of the Graetz family, the story about buying Castel di Vinciliata, her immediate plans to be at a dig in Turkey, and how pleased she is we bought one of Gidon's sculptures. Had we noticed its likeness at the end of the pathway and did it not look wonderful? . . . Oh, sorry, she must be off. She is preparing to go to Israel before she leaves for Turkey . . . Oh, we had been to Israel? When? And how did we enjoy it? Wonderful. We must let her entertain us when we return there again. She hopes we will come back to the castello. She knows Gidon wants to show us his studio. She drains her teacup and puts it on the table. She stands, shakes hands, saying to each of us, "goodbye 'til we meet again." With the black cape flapping behind, she swishes off.

For a few moments no one says a word. We are breathless. "Well," says Gidon, "that's my mother!" We laugh and start to enjoy our own tea.

℥

The Gerardo Krafts are the third generation of the family who have resided in Florence. Gerardo's grandfather grew up in Switzerland, then lived and worked in Florence as did his father. Gerardo is the third in his line to do the same. He is an Italian resident, but a Swiss citizen. His children, all Swiss citizens, were raised in Italy, but finished their education in Switzerland. The family are hoteliers by trade. They have built some of the most prestigious hotels in Europe. Currently, their son is in the business and doing a fine job.

℥

Smooth-shaven, round-faced Gerardo looks well fed. He is an energetic man, unwilling to sit on any sidelines. He is interested in the development of the commercial airport of Florence. He realizes its enlargement and improvements could bring more trade to the city. It is at the airport where we first met him. He does not want Florence to fall behind other Italian cities, business-wise. There is a distinct possibility this may happen. He loves knowing people and has many friends among the political hierarchy. He recently became the Swiss Consul. He always is promoting some sort of a deal with someone. Wearing a safety helmet he rides in and out of Florence on a small motorcycle. This saves him blocks of walking to the center of town where private cars are not allowed to drive.

＆

Gerardo and Karin, his vivacious German-born wife, thoroughly enjoy entertaining influential people in their home. It is a lovely place, although they claim it has need of many repairs. Somehow each time repairs are done, the house grows a bit larger. Italians frown on additions to houses as not being for the common good.

＆

The evening we are invited to dinner it is rainy and wet. We arrive by taxi and walk through the garden which is filled with an unusual display of many varieties of flowering azaleas in huge terracotta pots. It is a lovely welcoming in the misty rain. Karin is responsible for these beautiful plants. She is a talented gardener. We walk into the house and are introduced to several other couples, and Edgar and Caroline, the son and younger daughter of the Krafts. They will help serving the dinner. They tell us they are honored to be a part of the evening, and it is evident they will add much ambiance to the party. The people we meet are from varied nationalities and occupations. This group includes the retiring Swiss Consul and his American wife, a Russian couple, a Swiss artist and his wife, a Lithuanian couple, an Italian man and his American wife, and a few other Germans and Swiss. All of them have homes nearby. While sipping an aperitif, we stand and talk. It is informal and pleasant.

℃

Dinner and the rest of the evening is spent sitting around the huge dining room table. Edgar and Caroline pass the dinner plates on which their mother serves the food. They do so with dignity and obvious pride. We enjoy roast beef and small pieces of roast lamb, potatoes from Germany, (we receive much teasing about these being from Germany and not Idaho), a variety of fresh vegetables and salad greens from their garden, as well as condiments and sauces. Dessert is Edgar's specialty. He flambes crepes and serves these with a delicious custardy sauce he has concocted. We enjoy both red and white wines. The coffee tray is placed in front of Karin. With it we are offered liqueurs from an assortment of bottles in a variety of lovely antique decanters. We enjoy the rest of the evening with good conversation and a few frankly expressed opinions.

℃

From my end of the table:

"Do you think Mr. Reagan will win the election, Mrs. Whiting?"

"Oh, I don't know. Who can predict anything political? What do you think?"

"I'm certain he will lose," says the American wife of the Italian, very positively.

"When were you last in the United States?" I ask.

"A few months ago," she replies. Then she adds, "No one

would vote for a movie star!"

Pre-dinner gossip had it this American and her considerably younger Italian husband are enthusiastic communists. While this is not too surprising in Italy, I am amused how certain she is about the upcoming American election.

(It is a matter of record Ronald Reagan won that election by the greatest landslide victory of the century. So much for political predictions!)

᪥

Another discussion:

"Do you have children, Mrs. Whiting?" asks my dinner partner, the Swiss consul.

I reply Mac and I birthed and raised six.

"My God! How does one ever raise that many?" I am asked.

"Well, how many do you have?"

"Oh, none, thank the Lord. Never could have any, thank goodness. Never missed them either. We are entertaining my wife's niece and that's enough for me. She's unbearable. I'm going to send her home."

"Who's that?" I asked.

"Oh, my niece, of course. You didn't think I meant my wife. Couldn't do without her!"

᪥

There is an abnormal amount of noise outside our hotel window. This room in Milan faces the front of the hotel so we are overlooking its entrance driveway. We look out and see a small group of teenage girls gathered around. They are dressed in blue jeans and t-shirts. Some have cameras. All are looking our way. Some see us and point to our window.

"What in the world is happening?" we wonder aloud to each other. "Probably just a bunch of kids on their way home from school," we decide.

We go about unpacking as we have just arrived. We pay no more attention to outside, but the noise gets louder and louder. We go back to the window to look out. This time there is a larger crowd, most all of them girls. Seeing us, they yell!

"It's got to be some celebrity staying here," says Mac. "Why else would they be hanging around?"

"But, who is it?" say I, curiously.

"Darned if I know," answers Mac.

All afternoon the kids meander around the driveway entrance, alternately yelling, "Hey, --ee! Come out! Come out!" We could not understand who '--ee' is, not hearing the name. We think they might be saying Bob-bee or is it John-ee? We cannot decide. They are so loud two porters from the hotel go out and ask the crowd to quiet down. Briefly it does. A guest on our floor sticks his head out of his window to see what is all the commotion. The kids yell at him, "Hey, are you somebody?" Until then the guest always thought he was, but now he quickly pulls his head back inside wondering who he is supposed to be.

About six o'clock (after four hours of commotion!) a great huge shriek, "--ee" appears at his window. To our amazement "--ee" is directly below us! No wonder they watched when we looked out. The kids run up to the hotel directly under us. "We love you, --ee!" One girl in a lavender t-shirt runs forward her arms held out ready for an embrace, yelling, "I love you, --ee!" A mother with a group of little children, probably age six to eight years old, is on the other side of the driveway watching. They do not run up to the entrance, but the mother points so the little ones know where to look. These kids are interested, but not hysterical like the teenagers. "--ee" appears a couple of more times, teasing the crowd and building its anticipation of his arrival in the lobby, we guess. Hopefully he will not stay below us any longer than necessary. We realize this must be a male movie star or rock singer. Otherwise there never would be such a group of females.

"--ee's" car, a shining Mercedes jeep, is brought to the entrance so we watch to see who it is. Shrieks! Everyone dashes forward. Then, he appears. It's none other than Sylvester Stallone, Mr. Rambo himself! The kids had been yelling "Sly, Sly." All now is perfectly quiet around the entrance, surprisingly. Perhaps he is signing autographs. We cannot see what is happening. Finally he gets into the car, sitting in the back seat. As he slowly is driven out the driveway, the girls run after his car, banging on the windows, yelling they love him, many sobbing with excitement. He waves. The car leaves the drive and turns into the city traffic.

Eventually the crowd disperses. What an emotional display! Such a tiny-sized person, this Sylvester Stallone, who thrills his audiences playing big, macho Rambo. Hard to believe that little man caused such excitement. Some way to make a living, but what a living he has made!

It's not what you know, but who you know. Or does it only seem this way over here?

CHAPTER

14

Aₛ we meander through the countryside we drive to Rimini, San Remo, and as far away as Lugano and Milan. One of the most fascinating spots we discover is nearby, outside Castellina in Chianti, called Tenuta di Ricavo. We arrange to stay there for two nights. Upon arrival our Swiss hosts welcome us. We are the only Americans this weekend. Everybody else is German or Swiss.

Dinner is to be served at seven thirty with the men

245

requested to wear jackets. This is an unusual request since we are deep in the country. Suitably clothed we present ourselves at the proper time and are seated immediately. Although we are shown the menu, this is only to let us know what will be served.

℘

First comes the risotto—rice with clams, mussels, octopus and other bi-valves. It is good, if not excellent. The waiter presents the secondo piatto—a platter on which there are three squid, sauced with red wine. Not only does this not look attractive, we are not overly fond of squid. Looking around we notice none of the other guests seem to be happy with this entree either. There is no other accompaniment like, for instance, a vegetable or a green salad. Dessert is a combination of stewed prunes and apples, prugne e mele. Not having enjoyed the squid, indeed leaving it on the platter, we are hungry. One of us requests formaggio e pane, cheese and bread. How good that tastes. Coffee is served in the living room by a roaring fire. Both are most welcome.

An extraordinary evening—one of the few times we truly did not enjoy the Italian cuisine. Apparently, neither did anyone else. We never saw so many platters leave tables completely untouched. We were not the only unhappy diners. We suggest the chef had gotten an unusually good price for those squid, but it was not the most successful dinner for either him or his guests.

℘

The Tenuta di Ricavo was a farm hamlet dating back to early times. The definition of a tenuta is a little village or a collection of buildings and homes around an estate house. Riboia including our Poggio is another example. This tenuta has its original church, which is still used. Much of this land was owned by the same families for a period of time longer than the entire history of the United States, including the colonial period.

C

We understand in a tenuta all of the property belongs to the padrone, who lives in the villa on the estate. He shares the produce from the farm with the paesani, the peasants, who get fifty five percent of the yield under the system of mezzadria. At this tenuta the padrone got less than the usual half share because his land was so difficult to work.

C

In those early times the peasants probably started laboring at three in the morning before sunrise and toiled continuously until sunset. Water was carried from the stream far below up the hill to the village on top. There was no electricity, no water, and no heat in the village. All permanent possessions belonged to the padrone. What belonged to the padrone was not only the buildings, but the livestock and tools including the plows and vehicles. People who worked there knew no other existence. They survived by

247

pure drudgery and eked out a meager existence. They seldom had a choice of any alternative employment. It is these conditions that eventually prompted emigration to the United States, Australia, and other countries. It is also understandable why communism had an appeal for the people, la gente.

෬

The whole tax structure of Italy is tilted toward ownership of property staying in the same family. The family holds onto its stake and does not necessarily develop it into something new. This is thought to be the natural state of affairs. There is little pressure for people to work the land, making it pay for itself or else sell it to others. That is why there are so many run down villas. Land is not expensive to keep. Little, if any, tax is paid for its ownership, unlike in the United States. Land is expensive to sell because there is a huge tax paid on the sale. This encourages a static culture rather than a dynamic one. More and more people have moved off the land to work in city factories. They love the land, but need the good salaries from the factory jobs. There is little compensation for the hard labor of farming. This problem builds huge pressures among the politicians for land reform. The Italian Communist Party makes much capital from this. Meantime the land lays fallow year after year. For an economy which produces beautiful farm products, this is sad to see much less understand.

෬

The Tenuta di Ricavo is presently owned by a Swiss couple who took ownership after World War Two. This same family runs it today. It is interesting that the present owner worked in the United States for du Pont and Aerojet General before returning to Italy. This is one reason why he was so happy to see us. Faces from America!

§

Our delightfully old fashioned room with its original slanted stone floor and tiny shuttered windows, once probably held a family of six or eight people with their animals stalled below. Cooking was done in the fireplace, which is still there. It has stone seats inside on either side, obviously the warmest place to be seated in the room. There was no indoor plumbing. Now there is a large bathroom with all the modern conveniences.

§

"Throw a bundle on the fire!" We have a neat pile of bundles beside our fireplace at the Tenuta. Each bundle has the same size pieces of wood tied together. There are some bundles of straw, some of grass, some of small twigs, a few larger twigs, and two or three larger logs. When assembling the fire to burn, the bundles are not untied. They are arranged with the smallest on the bottom building up to the largest on top. When the fire is lit, it burns with vigor. Incidentally, each bundle is tied together in the middle with a piece of its own material.

We thoroughly enjoy this fireplace, which we are encouraged to light, watching each bundle ignite, one after another, into a blaze. Such a bundle is called fascia, the name from which the Fascist political party was derived. I sit in one of the inside seats. It is a bit smoky, bringing tears to my eyes, but it is warm and cozy so I close my eyes and enjoy being atmospheric.

*

I bought oak and chestnut honey at the Badia di Coltibuono's produce shop. Their olive oil and vinegar as well as wine is sold in the United States. I did not know they sold honeys before this visit.

The oak honey is unusual. As the sap flows from the oak tree, aphids consume the sap and convert it into sugar. Bees then collect the sugar from the aphids. They make it into honey.

*

We lunch at Castello di Spaltenna in Gaiole. Originally this was a convent perched high on a hill above the town of Gaiole. It has a spectacular view of the hilly landscape surrounding. Slowly the convent is being converted into a small hotel. There are few rooms available for guests now.

A beautiful luncheon is served to us in the old refectory, a handsome, high ceilinged, wooden beamed room with a huge fireplace dominating one end. There is one floor to ceiling window, and it fascinates us. It is oval shaped with huge wooden matching doors to cover it and overlooks an intimate courtyard where luncheon may also be enjoyed. One sits under huge white canvas umbrellas surrounded by blooming flowers. Such surroundings are good for the digestion, and our Irish host, once a chef at a former restaurant in Rome does not disappoint us nor any guest.

His wife designed the curtain material for the dining room inside. She hand printed huge pink and blue irises on an off-white material and made it into floor to ceiling curtains. They are beautiful. The tables are set with white tablecloths dotted with tiny blue flowers and white Irish linen overcloths. Both the flowers and seats of the chairs are a bright French blue, making a clean, fresh ambiance for a leisurely meal whether large or small.

One noon we enjoyed luncheon at the Castello di Spaltenna with our young granddaughter, Castine, and her mother. Since Castine was only two years old a highchair is brought to our table for her use. She was an extremely quiet little girl, but insisted on chewing her food sitting in the chair turned backwards so she could observe the table of diners next to us eating their meal. Her mother was not overjoyed with this behavior, and as soon as she finished, whisked Castine out of the room. Our Irish host saw us leaving and asked if we would like to visit their chapel. We had not realized it is the front wing of the entire structure.

Centuries of loving care shows in that chapel which probably dates from the twelfth century. It is tiny, seating at most a scant dozen or so people. It has a lovely stained glass window above the altar, and there is an ancient oriental rug running down the center aisle. There were bouquets of flowers scattered around from a wedding performed that weekend. This gives me an idea. I ask Castine if she likes to play "here comes the bride"? "I dooooo!" answers Castine, her voice rising several octaves, and her blue eyes blinking enthusiastically at me. I suspect she has not the vaguest idea what this game is about. So she and I make-believe. She is the bride, and I am the groom. Holding hands we solemnly march up the aisle to the altar, singing "here comes the bride." We pause for a moment at the altar to hear the vows, then, I whirl her around and singing the traditional wedding recessional song, "la da ti da da dada" as loud as we can, down the aisle we dash at a breathtaking speed. We are so enthralled how much fun this is that we play several more times before leaving the chapel.

☙

Castine is to be the flower girl at her aunt's wedding soon after she returns home. Hopefully our exuberance here helped set as joyous a mood for the real affair as was our fun playacting in this beautiful, little ancient chapel.

☙

252

Such girlish capering never appeals to our grandsons, Mac and Corey, while they are in Italy. They were happy hiking around the countryside to see what they could discover. One day they found a pheasant, sitting on a nest of eggs. The delicate shell of one egg had fallen onto the ground. It was gingerly carried back to our house by Corey for his mother to see. How proudly he handed it to her. Mac loved climbing an old cherry tree. He got into its branches from a rickety, old wooden homemade ladder. There he sat in the top of the tree. Totally contented, Mac picked and ate the fruit while he scanned the wonders of the countryside from this high perspective.

The grandest treat of all for the boys was an expedition into Florence to the science museum with their parents. In Italian it is called Museo Nazionale di Storia della Scienza, The National Museum of the History of Science. Among the treasures dazzling them the best one was the exhibition of Galileo, the astronomer. They could not wait to tell us a container held Galileo's finger, his middle finger, at that, and it was a very long finger too! At eight and four years of age what an impression this made.

"I belly we doe a sinister." Umberto, our Positano driver/guide is deciding which way to turn. Should he "belly doe a dexter, or belly directo?" (The decision is whether to turn right, left or keep going straight.)

He told us one night after he was in bed, his telephone rang. "Me wife, she ans the tel. I wast in bedded, but I talked to guy. He wast Los Angeles. He call all way to Posey! He vanto me go Veetree ask fello 'bout he purchase dishes. Seven hun doll worth—lot of mon. Why he not call directo hisself, directo Los Angeles to Posey?"

❧

Later:
"Say, Bister Whiting—why you talk so fun'? Where you learnt spake Italian dat way? Sure sound funny."

Giovanna, so proud of her Tuscan Italian, would have been horrified.

❧

Umberto is speaking what he calls good American. A native of Positano, it is doubtful his schooling was much more than two or three years. He learned his American from the soldiers during World War II.

❧

One of the wonders and horrors of driving through Naples is the sight of a solid stream of traffic going east with

254

one small car in the midst going west!

§

On really long drives we amused ourselves practicing counting in Italian. One of us would start by saying, uno, one, the other replies, due, two, and we would see just how far we could go. Our maximum achievement reached a thousand. That was on a long stretch of road and was quite enough counting for one session.

§

Greve is a small town with a square in its center where people meet and cars are parked. What makes it unusual is there is a loggia completely around the square. Underneath the loggia are the village stores. Above the loggia are balconies of apartments where the store owners live. These balconies are filled with terracotta pots planted with flowers which spill over the sides of the balconies. Whether by plan or by accident, there is an aura here which is inviting and very pretty.

§

Greve has an excellent enoteca, which is a shop that sells wine. One Wednesday afternoon we drove there to look over their assortment. The shop was closed. Other stores in the town were open so we did not understand why this one was not. To our surprise we learn all enotecas are closed every Wednesday afternoon. We are told grocery stores are too. All other stores close every Monday until three thirty in the afternoon. One tries hard to plan for all these little trivialities which have a way of upsetting the best laid plans!

ౡ

The Certosa di Maggino is as elegant a suburban inn as can be found anywhere in the world. Originally a monastery dating back to the twelfth century, it is situated just outside the walls of patrician Siena. The maids wear black uniforms with small lace aprons and headbands across their hair. Never would a Florentine maid allow herself to be regimented like that. It would offend her dignity.

ౡ

We have two rooms at the Certosa, a suite. The first is a small living room through which one walks to the bedroom and bathroom. To the left of the living room is a small, stainless steel kitchenette.

The living room is furnished with two day beds, used as sofas daytime and beds nighttime. Those along with a round table and two matching chairs are the furnishings although there is a small breakfront at the entrance to the suite. Both living room and bedroom are decorated with similar red fabric. This is used as wallpaper in both rooms as well as bedspreads and cushions on the chairs in the living room. The woodwork in both rooms is maple. It makes a pleasant combination with all the fabric. There are two windows in the living room, which can be opened by throwing back their shutters. The view is the newly started gardens of our neighbors. In that neighborhood, we soon found out, is a rooster who did not mind crowing as soon as the sun comes up. Such a contrast to city living!

※

There are other birds at the Certosa besides the rooster. They are early risers too. The first one up sings a solo and that lulls us into napping. Shortly he is joined by a second bird, and this is a duet. Then a trio follows, and its quite pleasant. Soon, however, it becomes a symphony as dozens and dozens join the chorus. Now we definitely wake up! No late sleepers in this countryside.

※

Divieto di Caccia says the sign all along the road. No hunting here it means although some do not pay heed.

※

The duomo, cathedral, in Orvieto is one of the prettiest in all of Italy. We had been told not to miss seeing it so we drive through the walled city looking for it.

The old city is full of wonderful twisty, narrow streets. Some are so narrow a single car is all that can go through at one time. We are on such a street when we get our first glimpse of the duomo. Compared to the buildings on either side of us, the duomo is enormous. It sits in a square, completely alone, with lots of space around it. This emphasizes its size.

℅

We are able to park only with difficulty, not many spots being available. Not immediately noticing where the front of the duomo is, we see a bus with people from it going in an open door along a side of the church. We assume this is the way to enter so we tag along. Imagine our surprise as we join the group to find them handicapped people, many in wheel chairs. The look of pure joy on their faces as each enters the duomo is a pleasure for the rest of us to see.

℅

When we finish visiting inside, we decide to walk around outside. The front of this church is a sight to behold, graced with slender delicate spiral columns of marble. The niches behind these are worked in mosaic of many blue shades. The entrance doors are huge—both in height and width and are crafted in bronze. There are statues in the niches on either side. It is altogether an overwhelming wealth of beauty. We look and feel a sense of awe.

☙

When it is finally time to go, we slowly walk down the steps to the street. We are reluctant to leave. Suddenly four or five young teenage boys dash by us, running up to the bronze doors. One boy carries a large ghetto blaster. He sets it down beside the door and turns up its volume. Loud rock and roll music erupts. The boys dance a bit and yell back and forth over its booming volume.

This upsets us. They have totally broken the tranquillity. What disregard for a religious building. There is no feeling of reverence for what the building represents nor recognition it is a place of great beauty. They crave a different kind of gratification and that is what they are getting. We shake our heads and leave, wishing they had found another spot for their exuberance.

☙

We drive to Arezzo to see the Church of St. Francis, arriving at five minutes to twelve. We are pleased to see one o'clock is the posted closing time. At exactly twelve the sexton appears from somewhere deep inside the church and announces we must leave. He is closing the church. We protest to no avail even taking him outside to read the sign. He wants to close the church, and he does!

🜲

We have had the same thing happen other places. We wanted to see Castel di Romana. Arrived there at twelve fifteen. We found the castle was not open from twelve to three in the afternoon.

Another time when we stopped at Castel di Meleto for our fourth attempt to visit it, there is a tour group inside. We are not allowed to enter because we had not made a previous appointment three months in advance!

And so it is apt to go when one sightsees here. It can be very frustrating.

🜲

I am puffing up a side of one of the many bridges in Venice when, at the top, pausing for a breath, I hear the click of a camera. I look to my left and see the lens of a camera pointed directly at my legs!

Of the multitude of sights in that captivating city worth recording, and hoards of every type tourist invented by the Good Lord to look at, why me?

"Well, why not?" says Mac.

🜲

The ebullience and creativity of the Italians would be intolerable except for the moderating influence of the bureaucracy which succeeds in stopping almost every action.

&

The Germans have a natural guilt complex about Hitler, but the Italians have ambiguous feelings about Mussolini. They knew he could never maneuver an ethnic incineration, and they look back with some nostalgia on the days when some trains ran on time.

&

A rocca is a medieval tower. They stand tall on the high hills throughout the Italian landside. They are structures made of stone, starkly plain in design, and look handsome against the landscape. They were built to use as signal towers in the early days. One tower would signal its nearest neighbor who would pass the message along to the next rocca. Thus enemies were spotted and towns could get ready. The enemy did not take a town by surprise.

&

A final translation from La Nazione by Mac:

Paris. Policemen, platoons of lawyers in robes, a few Italian journalists in the chambers, the first appearance at the court of Paris. We are here to be present at the first interrogation of Michele Zaza, boss of the Camorra, arrested last Sunday as he came out of a luxury apartment in the most chic quarter of the city, a few steps away from the Place de L'Etoile.

"But of 'Crazy Mike', no trace: his first in settlement of the few formalities, to attest that there has arrived from Italy the file with the request for extradition.

"The mistake which caught newspapers and press services of Paris must have been caused by the fact that the first name in the list of persons to appear before the judges was that of a Jugoslav, Djasar (pronounced in French much like 'Zaza'). A poor wretch accused of theft, who had never expected to see such a crowd in the courtroom. There was a bit of turmoil when the judge asked that an interpreter of Slavic be present. There was in compensation an Italian interpreter. She was persuaded as well to see in handcuffs the Camorra boss, and despairing for the journalists she said, 'What will I do if the boss starts speaking Neapolitan?'

"Michele Zaza was not far from the palace of justice. As he suffers from a heart condition, he has been admitted to the coronary ward of the hospital 'Hotel Dieu,' a short hundred meters away. It is the oldest hospital of Paris, and the coronary ward is a veritable Fort Knox, with barred doors and windows, police at every juncture, and connected with the outside only by way of an elevator which leads to an underground tunnel. It would be most difficult for the king of escapists to succeed in escaping here."

The time is early July 1980. Our three months lease at Poggio Ramerino and stay in the Excelsior Hotel have ended. We are packed and ready to fly back to the United States. The drive to the airport is full of both nostalgia and joy for we have had a wonderful time here, but we will be happy to be in our own country and home.

$$\mathscr{E}$$

The airport security at Peretola is quite casual so one does not have to be escorted to one's airplane by an official. I am heading toward ours by myself, while Mac finishes some business in the terminal. Out of the corner of my eye I note a stylish, white-haired gentleman a little way behind. He looks very dapper, dressed in a tan polo coat with a white scarf casually thrown around his neck. He walks with a jaunty stride and appears to be trailing me. I am anxious to get to the plane and only give him a fleeting glance. I walk rapidly with a lively, energetic pace.

I reach the plane, greet our pilot, and climb aboard. I am more than happy to lay down the purse, tote bag, book and coat which I had been carrying. I turn toward the back of the cabin and start stowing away these belongings. I hear someone climbing aboard, and assuming it is Mac, turn to greet him. To my utter surprise there stands a complete stranger, the man in the polo coat. He was following me!

Dumbfounded I say, "Hello, who are you?"

"Never mind," he answers in Italian-accented English. "Is OK. You sit down," he motions to me.

"Sir," I bristle, not sitting down, "what do you want? This is not your aircraft." The ugly vision of hijacking quickly passes through my mind. Is this happening right now? To me?

"No, no, sit down! I have ticket here." Impatiently he jams his hand into his right coat pocket.

At the same time I hear our pilot come aboard. He is checking who this individual might be. The man is not listed as a passenger on the flight manifest for this trip. Alan has no idea a drama is taking place, and I do not greet him. Instead I am spellbound watching for a hand to emerge from a coat pocket. To myself I think, "Well, this man is either going to pull out a nice little ticket or an ugly little gun. I'll surely know in a second." I am more annoyed at the intrusion of my privacy than afraid of any possible consequences. The hand jerks out of the pocket and thrusts forward toward my face. Clearly I see a piece of paper which, of course, is an airline ticket. "Oh, thank God!" I say to myself. I turn toward Alan. He still has no idea what has been transpiring. "Would you mind helping this man find his airplane, Al? I think he is lost."

"No, no," says Alan, seeing the ticket. He smiles at the man and says, "Your airplane is over there." He points to an airliner on the other side of the field.

The confused man insists we are his airliner. If we are not, where is his? He does not understand. Alan gently takes him by the arm and leads him off onto the tarmac. He bodily positions him in the direction where he can observe his airliner boarding passengers. Now the man sees it is on the other side of the field. Walking with his jaunty stride he leaves.

ᘓ

This episode abruptly reminds me of the safety problem at this time in Italy and might have ended tragically. I had almost forgotten hi-jackings and kneecappings are still happening so content and fulfilled our life has been living our adventure in this lovely country.

265

Alan comes back aboard. We look at each other and laugh. Shrugging our shoulders we say simultaneously, "Well, that's Italian!"

Arrivederci!

EPILOGUE

The Poggio was sold in the mid-eighties to an Italian industrialist from Prato. We were notified it was for sale by the real estate agent who originally rented it to us. She wrote asking if we wished to buy it. Sentimentally we might have done so. Realistically it was not a good investment for us. There are so many restrictions owning property in Italy that it is not worth our time trying to decipher them. We concluded we do not want to live in Italy, but we will make frequent and extended visits very often.

We went by the property on a recent trip and found it somewhat changed. The fencing along via di Riboia was removed so anyone can see the yard inside. The wonderful mystery of what was there is forever gone.

The big house at the end of the road, the original Riboia villa, is undergoing restoration. This is exciting.

We understand the Poggio owners from whom we rented, after realizing a profit from selling the Poggio, are looking around for another property in Tuscany.

༄

From our experience at the Poggio Italy became an important part of our life, and we shall think of it as our second home. Italians have the capacity for making visitors feel welcome. They share their own feelings and are sensitive to the feelings of others. They accept the idiosyncracies of people, and they are not ashamed to expose their own. They cherish family more than any social relationship. And, nobody ever understands just why, but it is accepted Italians live better than almost anyone.

༄

Dilia and her family moved away from the Poggio. We assume they are living nearer where Sante works. We often think of Dilia's many kindnesses to us. Massimo with his black eyes and unruly hair must be a teenager now. We remember his vivid imagination and how he loved to tease i gatti. We expect he is doing well in school.

We enjoy using their espresso pot!

༄

Our friend Frederick Hand died driving a mo-ped. He stopped at a traffic light. While waiting for it to turn green, he put his foot down on the cobblestone street to light a cigarette. He slipped and fell, striking his head. He was not wearing a safety helmet. He never recovered from the coma he suffered. An ignominious way for a chauffeur to die after a career of driving more than a million miles in highly powered automobiles.

༄

The Fenyes family continue living their suburban life. Alberto retired from the United States Consulate. Didi finished his military service and married his long-time girl friend. Their daughter was born shortly thereafter. They live in the front room of the Fenyes home while he finishes studying for his law degree. Mimma works at Peretola Airport and receives high praise for the professional job she does there from everyone. (Her father thinks she has much too much responsibility for such a young person!) She currently dates a pilot but plans no serious commitment.

Our Giovanna stays at home and takes care of them, plus all the stray cats in the neighborhood. She has not been able to stop smoking, and this has caused heart damage. She is impatient with her inactive life.

༄

Then, in March of 1989 this letter arrived from Adalberto:

Dearest Helen and Mac,

It is with deep sorrowness that I have to inform you, dear friends, of the death of Giovanna on February 25. She passed away without suffering in the hospital where she had been admitted on the 8th of February. It went fast. The lung cancer, which was discovered mid-October, did work rapidly and destroyed totally her liver and kidneys.

Even if Giovanna was practically disabled for the last year and a half, and, of course, could not take care of any house care, it is hard to resettle our lives. Thank God our little grandchild keeps us busy. Didi, Mimma, Lorenza and myself are forming a good team: we share our duties and we come along quite good, but the loss is still unbearable.

We are all looking forward to seeing you in the spring and I'll then tell you more about the tragedy.

Our love to all of you.

Adalberto

🙖

Mac and I are just devastated by this letter.

🙖

Peretola Airport, serving Florence with its single runway has been modernized, and its terminal is enlarged. It manages several commercial airlines which bring in people directly from all parts of Europe as well as flying them out.

Its terminal has a waiting room off to one side that is

handsomely tiled and decorated with black leather Barcelona style lounge chairs. There are also terracotta pots of green plants in various corners. This is far different from the gray colored, wooden benched cold reception room where we used to be greeted by the customs officials. In another section a small cafeteria as well as a newsstand are available. There are even two rent-a-car windows with automobiles immediately available outside the front entrance.

Plenty of taxis await customers too. How short a time ago it was when Mac had to telephone for this service upon our arrival. It was always an immediate test to see how much Italian he had remembered!

All this must delight Gerardo Kraft who worked so hard to make it possible.

℡

Karin and Gerardo Kraft are planning the first family wedding, that of their younger daughter, Caroline. The elder daughter, Alexandra, is becoming a physician. The son, Edgar, runs the family hotel efficiently. Gerardo continues to take an active interest in everything in Tuscany.

℡

We think the Excelsior Hotel still the best in Florence. Their staff remains outstanding. Some of its personnel was moved across the street to the newly opened Grand Hotel. Labor disputes finally at an end, this hotel is gradually reopening its rooms to the tourist trade.

❧

The impersonators who entertained us with their nightly antics in the parking square between the two hotels are still amusing everyone. There is the same screeching of brakes, when, turning the corner, drivers confront these sights. They are part of the ambiance.

❧

Italian driving is as crazy as ever. Somehow it bothers neither of us at all. We expect it as part of the scene. Mac enjoys its challenge. Once adjusted to the tempo Italian-style, it is fun. I do not sit in the back seat anymore. I might miss something interesting!

❧

Florence proper has many more restrictions about where cars can be driven and parked. None are allowed into the inner city. Some of this is to help clear the air which was getting too polluted as well as an attempt to control a too large volume of traffic cruising through the city. At certain hours no vehicles are allowed to drive along the Arno either. It is almost easier to take taxis than bother with an automobile.

❦

Pollution remains a major problem both in the cities and countryside. Still allowed is the burning of olive prunings which the farmers do whenever they have enough to create a significant fire. Once ignited those branches make billows of smoke which flows upward, then covers the entire countryside with a blanket of greyness.

One wonders why the environmentalists do not protest.

❦

And us? We have our Souvenirs of Tuscany, and we have just rented a lovely villa for two months. It is in the countryside near the small city of Pontassieve. We plan to bring our grandbabies so they can begin to appreciate Italy too. There will be a few language lessons for them (Granny may join the class!) and some cooking ones for their mothers. Since Mac is fluent in Italian, there is no need for more long hours spent studying. That time we shall fill enjoying the flowers and the sunshine and the food sightseeing with our family. We will luxuriate in the environment and getting a fresh look at everything Italian through their eyes.

GLOSSARY

To help understand some of the Italian words and phrases used.

A

allora - well, then
ancora - yet, still, even, more, again
anno - year
antipasto - hors d'oeuvre
aperto - open
apres vous - (French) after you
arredi - odds and ends, furnishings
arredi sacri - sacred vessels and vestments
arrivederci - goodbye, 'til we meet again
aspetta! - listen!
autostrada - superhighway
avanti - Come in!

B

bambini - children
basta - enough
Belli Arte - Department of Fine Arts
bellissimo - most beautiful
bene - good, well
benissimo - best, excellent, very good
bianco - white
bietola - beet greens
biscotini - cookies, biscuits
bottiglia - bottle
bravo - good, clever
buona sera - good evening

B

buon giorno - good morning
burro - butter

C

caldo - hot
cantina - cellar
caramelle - candy
carnesecche - dry meat
casa - house
casa colonica - farmhouse
castello - castle
certamente - certainly
certosa - Carthusian monastery
Che tempo fa? - What is the weather like?
chi - who
chiesa - church
chiuso - closed
ciao - hi! bye bye, so long
ciccina - fat lady
ciliegie - cherries
cipressi - cypress trees
Ci vuola una ricevuta. - I need a receipt.
Ci vuole dieci galloni. - I need ten gallons.
colazione - lunch
Come si dice? - How do you say?
Come va? - How are you?
con - with
coniglio - rabbit
contadini - country folk, peasants

D

destra - right-hand
distratto - absent-minded
dizionario - dictionary
dogana centrale - main office of customs
dolci - sweets
domani - tomorrow
dopo - after
dove - where
Dove lo sgabello? - Where is the stool?
due - two
duomo - cathedral

E

e - and
enoteca - wine shop
espresso - coffee

F

Fa bel tempo. - The weather is beautiful.
fattoria - farm
fetta - slice
fett'unta - oiled slice (of bread)
finito - finished
fiori - flowers
fiori di campo - flowers of the field
Firenze - Florence
formaggio - cheese
frantoia - oil press
freddo - cold

G

gallo - rooster
gamba - leg
gatta - female cat
gatto - male cat
ghiaccio - ice
giallo - yellow
giorno - day
giugno - June
grande - large
grande fagiolo - big bean
grazie - thank you
grazie tanto - thank you very much
gulfo - owl

I

ieri - yesterday
insalata verde - green salad
io - I
io sono - I am
italiano/inglese - Italian/English

L

lezione uno - lesson one
limoni - lemons
lira - Italian money denomination
lui - him

M

macchina da scrivere - typewriter
ma ma - but, maybe yes, maybe no
mamma mia - good gracious!

M

marito - husband
mele - apples
melone - melon
mercoledi - Wednesday
mezzadria - sharecrop system
moglie - wife
molto - very
molto bello - most beautiful
molto bene - very good
motorini - motorscooters

N

noi - we
non - no
non lei - no, you
nonna - grandmother
nonno - grandfather
notte - night
nuovo - new

O

olio di oliva - olive oil

P

padrone - master
pane - bread
pane di campagna - country
    bread
panino - roll
panna - cream
Parlo italiano. - I speak Italian.
pasta - noodles, an Italian
    staple which comes in
    dozens of different shapes,
    sizes, thicknesses, patterns

P

per favore - please
piatto primo - first course
piatto secondo - second course
piccolo - small
piccolo fagiolo - little bean
pini - pine trees
piselli - peas
po' d'olio - a little olive oil
poggio - hill
polizia - police
ponte - bridge
Ponte Vecchio - old bridge in
    Florence
Porta Romana - Roman gate
posta - mail
pranzo - dinner
prego - Not at all! Don't
    mention it! Please!
prima colazione - breakfast
pronto - ready
prosciutto - ham
prugne - prunes

Q

quando - when
quanto basta - as much as is
    sufficient

R

risotto - rice dish
rocca - fortress

S

salsiccia - sausage

277

S

San Pellegrino - brand of
    sparkling water
scarpe - shoes
sciopero - strike
scuola - school
scuolabus - schoolbus
scusi - sorry
settimana - week
si - yes
signor - gentleman, Mr.
signora - lady, Mrs.
signore - sir
signori - ladies, gentlemen
sinistra - left
spinaci - spinach
strada - road
stufa elettrica - electric heater
stupido - stupid, dumb

T

tenuta - estate, farm
terminato - finish
trattoria - restaurant
troppo freddo - too cold
tutto - all
tutto Firenze - all of Florence

U

un momento - just a moment

V

va bene - all right, OK
vape - vaporizer machine
vecchio - old
vengo - I'm coming
via di Riboia - street Riboia

V

vigili urbani - city police force
villa - country home with
    grounds
vino - wine
vino bianco Antinori - Antinori
    white wine
volere - to want
Vuole una tazza di caffe? - Do
    you want a cup of coffee?

NOTES AND ACKNOWLEDGEMENTS

This book was started as a series of jottings on my electric typewriter with its European keyboard, the macchina da scrivere, in the Pigeon's Roost at the Poggio during our lease. I cut those notes into segments and stapled each onto an index card. To see if I could make some sort of pattern out of them I made subject headings and filed the cards wherever they belonged under those topics. It was a total surprise to see what a pile had accumulated. I began to believe there was a book in the making.

At Mac's suggestion I transposed all my notes into WordStar files on his Otrona computer. This is the first time I ever used a computer. I was intrigued with the scope of work that could be accomplished. It was fun and so much easier for my kind of writing than the typewriter. Starting with that experience I became a firm computer enthusiast.

From the Otrona the files went onto my IBM PC. Then one Christmas Mac gave me a Toshiba T3100. All files came off the IBM onto the Toshiba. This is my machine. I love using it. I am never without it, and since it is light in weight and small in size, I personally carry it on every trip we make. It has dual voltage so is functional anywhere we may travel in the world.

In the beginning I learned the WordStar word processing program to use for the text and corrected my spelling with CorrectStar. The Thesaurus from WordPerfect was particularly helpful too. I then decided I needed my text double-spaced for easier editing. The WordPerfect program had this facility. (Mac had been urging me to update my files into WordPerfect so this was the time to learn that program.) There is a way to convert files from WordStar to Word-Perfect. It takes some practice and patience to learn, but it does work. After placing the entire text into WordPerfect

files, a single huge file was made so the book could be printed in one continuous process. My text is also on a three and a half inch disc. In this form it was presented to my publisher.

Hours and hours of work have gone into developing this manuscript. It was worked on in spurts and bounds in Sun Valley, whenever there was time, but more frequently when we traveled and no domestic demands competed for my attention. I have enjoyed the pleasure of writing in many places and countries. I would like to mention how pleasant it is for me to write at the Survetta House in St. Moritz, Switzerland. While Mac skis, I sit in our sunshine filled room and luxuriate writing.

The book is finished, at long last, at my desk in Sun Valley, Idaho. This is the appropriate place for it to end . . .

I am so pleased to have the help of Tinka Raymond, of Typographics in Ketchum, Idaho, and her excellent staff, in the production of this book.

The photographs were taken by Mac and me. The front cover photo is by Ethan Solosky.